The Show Matters

Inspiring Ideas to Ignite Hope, Wonder & Imagination in Your Classroom

Written by
Andrew Ntzouras, M.Ed.
Preston Trebas
Nate Mercuro

Illustrated by
AJ Zadravecz
(Former student of
Mr. N. and Mr. Trebas)

ISBN 978-0-578-62155-5

Library of Congress Control Number:2019920330

© 2019

Cover and Manuscript design by Aubrey BJork
Cover Art by AJ Zadravecz

SCENES

Acknowledgments

—

We would like to express our sincere gratitude to the following people who inspired us to create this book, and to those who have helped us along the way.

First and foremost, our families. To our parents who have inspired us to become the people we are today. Thank you! To our wives and children who have not only motivated and encouraged us, but also endured our absence over the many working hours and days. We love and appreciate you!

A huge shout out to the following people who donated their time, energy, and effort to help breathe life into our vision in the form of what we believe to be our manuscript and philosophy about teaching: David Banks, Ken Killian, Iris Martin, Suzanne Lynch, and Becky Trebas.

Another special thank you to Angela Stowe for initially planting the seed in our minds to write this book in the first place. None of this would have happened without that email.

Finally, to our managing editor, manuscript Jedi, and cover design wizard: Aubrey Bjork. Words truly fail us when attempting to express our gratitude. You are simply magical.

To all of our current, former, and even future students, this is because of you. This is for you.

And now, on with the show.

The Cast
Andrew Ntzouras M.Ed.
It's OK to Care

—

Thank you for taking the time to read this book. My name is Andrew Ntzouras, and I'm a public-school teacher in Mission Viejo, California. I began my career in teaching after earning my BA in History and Political Science and Multiple-Subject Teaching Credential from Vanguard University in Costa Mesa, California. Upon earning my credential, I substitute taught grades K-12 in Newport-Mesa Unified School District (NMUSD) for close to two years. During that time, I was a long-term substitute for various classes across the district. Soon, I was hired in NMUSD as a full-time fourth grade teacher. During that time, I also earned my M. Ed. with a focus on curriculum design, assessment, and instruction. The past five years I've spent teaching fourth and fifth grade at a charter school in South Orange County, California. Additionally, I serve as an adjunct professor at Vanguard University teaching Introduction to Education and

Integrating Technology into Classroom Teaching.

When I was a student in elementary school, I struggled. I didn't have high self-esteem. I always thought that everyone else was smarter than I was. In short, I didn't believe in myself. It wasn't until high school that I discovered that it was my attitude toward school that was the primary cause for my lack of success. I also had a wide variety of teachers who helped me believe in myself. They caused me to work hard and accomplish many academic achievements in their classes. Mr. Gautreau pushed me to write two 10-page research papers. I was challenged by Mrs. Sterger to work hard and solve complicated mathematical equations in her Algebra II class; my first and only A I ever earned in any math class. In Ms. Bean's class, I was motivated to turn in high-quality English reports—even when she sometimes would assign multiple projects at once. She believed in me, like all of her students, and instilled in us the strong work-ethic we needed to accomplish our dreams. In Ms. Van Fossen's Advanced Placement English class, I carefully analyzed Jane Eyre, Shakespeare, and developed the skills necessary to write strong opinioned essays with well-constructed arguments supported by research and facts. In college, I was inspired by professors that connected with their students. These men and women all made us feel valued and that our ideas had worth and meaning. They were able to do this because in short, they cared. They cared to make learning interesting. They cared that their students were successful. They cared about their respective fields of study. They cared that in the end they left their students better off and more prepared to pursue our own passions.

Before that path of academic success was illuminated, however, my original outlook on school negatively impacted my ability to even envision success in the classroom. In fact, I nearly failed sixth grade. My parents had to take me out of school and home school me throughout junior high. I completed an Independent Study Program for seventh and eighth grade. During this time, I worked on my studies at home, while opting to take some electives on campus. One of those electives allowed me to be a teacher's aide for a combo class for 1st and 2nd grade students. It was there that I discovered my passion for teaching and working with children. I began to realize that I could make an impact in the lives of others, and that my words and actions had meaning. I began to feel a sense of pride and satisfaction in bringing out the best in these kids. In high school, my grades began to get much better and in college, due in large part to the inspirational teachers and professors I had, I finally began to succeed academically and saw myself as smart and talented.

From nearly failing sixth grade to earning my BA with a 3.5 GPA and a 3.9 for my M.Ed., I'm confident that none of this would have been possible without the many teachers and professors who all shared one especially important belief: it's OK to care.

Now in my own class, I work hard each and every day to demonstrate that it is OK to care. I hope that after reading our book, you'll be even more inspired and motivated to be the best teacher you can for each and every one of your students that have the unique pleasure and opportunity of entering your class.

The best is yet to come,
Andrew Ntzouras

The Cast

Preston Trebas

"People won't care how much you know, until they know how much you care."

Teddy Roosevelt

—

If you were to ask me at different stages in my life what I wanted to be when I grew up, one profession you would never have heard was teacher. I wanted to grow up and become the president, a stockbroker, a professional baseball or football player, or a drummer in a punk rock band to name a few. Even when I started going to college at Brigham Young University in 2009, I wanted to become an oral surgeon. After serving a two-year mission for my church in the Philippines, I wanted to travel the world as a businessman and entrepreneur. It wasn't until I took an aptitude test in 2011 that I discovered my passion and calling was teaching.

While it took me awhile to discover that I was put on this Earth to teach, I had great examples of stellar educators, as well as wonderful examples of uninspiring and dream-crushing teachers. Both sides of this teacher coin somewhat brought me to where I am today: a sixth-grade teacher. It was my own sixth grade teacher, a giant of a man with a huge heart who showed us angsty, soon-to-be-teenagers, that education was important and that we mattered. If you were to ask any student in Mr. C.'s class who his favorite student was, everyone would respond that it was him or her; that's the type of teacher Mr. C. was.

I strive every day to make Mr. C. proud, trying to do for others what he did for me. I also had teachers in high school that eventually drove me to drop out of high school. I took my education into my own hands, learning what I wanted to learn. I didn't waste my time with these high school teachers that clearly didn't care about me. I eventually got my G.E.D. and even started taking flying lessons when I was 17. My experiences in high school taught me that children can easily tell when a teacher does not care if they pass or fail. So, I removed myself from the equation.

Today, even though my "job" is to educate the future generation, it rarely feels like work. I absolutely love what I do. I love helping students discover the joy of learning as I share my passion with them. I personally love music, playing guitar and drums, video games, and spending time in nature. I bring these passions into the class through music, fun and interactive games, and lessons with a focus on the bigger picture: the world.

I will admit that making the most of the world is really the driving force in my life. My own experiences in the world, both good and bad, eventually led me to joining the other millions of professionals that choose to sit in a room with 30+ screaming kids, determined to help them see and experience the world. It may seem like an impossible task to change the world, but we can sure change the world for our students.

Cheers!
Preston Trebas

The Cast

Nate Mercuro

Can't Never Did Anything, Try Did It All

—

They are ubiquitous phrases thrown around each and every week. You see them in memes. They pop up on social media. You hear them from friends and co-workers. "Ugh, Monday. I hate Mondays." "I don't want to go back to work tomorrow." "Is it Friday yet?"

I can totally relate. Or, I should say, I used to totally relate. This is how I felt about school as a kid. This is how I felt about work for years and years until I made a career change and discovered my true passion, teaching. As I discuss later in this book, I began my career in finance after graduating with a degree in Business Administration from California State University, Fullerton. First, working for a large corporation, and later starting and growing my own finance business. However, I didn't enjoy it. I wasn't excited about the industry as the days were long, and I didn't exactly look forward to going to work. I believe I actually learned to live this way back in elementary school. School wasn't exciting. I didn't enjoy it. And I certainly didn't look forward to going. From my experience then, and what I still see today, this is the viewpoint of the vast majority of kids. They find school boring, and long, with a ton of busy work beating them down even further. They can't wait for the weekends, they can't wait for their holidays, and certainly can't wait for their summer vacation. For many, it seems to start at this elementary school age, and then the pattern continues right into the working world.

Thomas Edison said, "I never did a day's work in my life. It was all fun." This is exactly how I feel now. I put in more effort at this calling than anything else I've ever done. But I'm having a blast, and absolutely love it. Never have I felt like I am just "working". It's challenging to me, it's inspiring to me, it's rewarding, it's fun. Because of this, in the six years I've taught, not once have I dreaded a Monday morning or uttered the words "Is it Friday yet?"

All of this is the driving force behind what I do for my classes each day and each year. What would my 9 or 10-year-old self think of my class and my lessons? What would I want my own children to experience in their classes? What is going to raise the engagement level through the roof and create the unforgettable experience for my students that ignites the same passion, drive, and motivation that I have for the profession of teaching? Students will want to work harder, and they will love what they are doing. Their curiosities will be piqued. Their passions will be ignited. They will be inspired!

Nate Mercuro

Pre-Production

"Some men see things as they are, and ask why. I dream of things that never were, and ask why not."

Senator Robert F. Kennedy

—

We believe that teaching should be inspiring. Teachers should inspire and be inspired. We believe that teachers should enjoy going to work each day. We believe that there is a fulfillment that comes from teaching that is unlike any other profession. Here is the thing.

Teaching is hard. It's not easy.

In fact, sometimes it seems the mission we are called to accomplish is nearly impossible. The profession's demands are insurmountable.

Here are some startling facts from the United States Department of Education:

-One-third (33.33%) of current public-school teachers do not expect to be teaching in K-12 schools five years from now.

-Of teachers who left teaching in 2008-09, about 40.8 percent of public school teachers reported opportunities for learning from colleagues (peer-to-peer professional development) were better in their current position than in teaching.

-Two of three Americans would like their child of to become a public school teacher, but are concerned that their local public schools are having a hard time getting good teachers. Americans say they hear more negative stories than positive stories about teachers from the news media.

According to the National Center for Education Statistics (NCES):

-About 51 percent of public school teachers who left teaching in 2012–13 reported that the manageability of their work load was better in their current position than in teaching.

-Research suggests that teachers in their first three to five years of the profession who are satisfied with their preparation and who receive support as they transition into the profession are less likely to exit the profession early (DeAngelis, Wall, and Che, 2013).

-Early career support is associated with improvements in teacher effectiveness (Henry, Bastian, and Fortner, 2011).

-New teachers who feel supported in their school environment may be more likely to stay in their school and in teaching than those without similar supports (Johnson and Birkeland, 2003).

Now the good news.

What if we showed you that teaching could be all that you ever hoped and dreamed it would be? You know what we're talking about. How you dreamed it would be when you first started your credential program.

What if we could convince you your dream of becoming a life-changer is waiting to come true?

It is.

The paperwork, we admit, may never end. This we can't promise to change. However, what if the papers, essays, and assignments you receive from your students are so incredibly impressive that you actually look forward to grading them?

What if we told you that you don't have to receive angry parent emails? Instead, you could receive emails and letters of gratitude. Emails and notes so full of praise and admiration that, after reading them, you would swear must have been addressed to someone like Kobe Bryant or Taylor Swift.

What if we told you that it's not too late to be that teacher that will change the world? That, dear reader, is exactly what we are telling you.

You can change the world.

It CAN be done.

Not only can you change the world, you can change it many times over. You can change the worlds of literally hundreds and perhaps thousands of students. You are a world changer. That's why you entered this profession in the first place.

The ideas you will find within this book have dramatically changed the way we teach. It all began with a text message group we started back in 2016. We exchanged ideas that we found to be working in the classroom. Ideas would just pop into our minds and somehow encourage wonder in the hearts and minds of our students.

These ideas just kept coming, and we kept sharing them. Soon, we noticed that the bell would ring and our students didn't want to leave. Students who once hated reading in previous years now tell us they love books and can't stop reading on the weekend. The students who hated writing now enthusiastically fill the pages of their writing journals with words that then fill their parents' eyes with tears of joy and amazement. Students who thought they would never be good at math now eagerly raise their hands in the classroom hoping for the chance to be the one to answer the question in front of the class.

Our purpose in writing this book is to help as many teachers as possible gain from our collective experiences in the classroom. We have found that teaching can be an isolating job. We've seen that often times, once fully employed as a teacher, the opportunities for true professional development and learning from other professionals seems to diminish, if not disappear entirely.

We want to change that.

In writing this book, we want to create a community of teachers that will help bring out the best in one another, share ideas, and continually refine our skills to be the best we can for our students.

This book is just the beginning.

Be sure to join us at theshowmatters.com and share your ideas. Join the national conversation. Together, we are stronger. Together, we can start a movement that embraces change, inspiration, and an obsession for great teaching.

All this, and more, can be done by embracing one philosophy:

The Show Matters.

Get ready for an unforgettable experience that just may change your whole life and the lives of all your students.

-Andrew Ntzouras, Preston Trebas, Nate Mercuro

Class Environment

"I do feel the classroom environment was different, and I liked this because it made me feel calm and peaceful at some points, but strong, happy, and upbeat at other times. Mr.N played music when we walked in and out, and throughout the day. Around the classroom, there were quotes on the walls, lights everywhere, and music playing. When I shared my journals, I got to use a microphone! This environment was incredibly fun and I loved this experience."

-Hailey
Former 4th Grade Student of Mr. Ntzouras

Fun

"I would say that I had more fun in Mr. Mercuro's class than any of my other years at my school. Mr. Mercuro had something new for us students everyday. I especially loved when we did Math Dodgeball. Mr. Mercuro just had a way of knowing how to make the lessons interesting, creative, and hands-on. I have so many other reasons why this year was so memorable and fantastic."

-Alyssa
Former 4th Grade Student of Mr. Mercuro

The Show Matters

"It's our stage, so
let's put on a good show."

Michael Eisner

—

Before I switched careers to teaching, I was in sales—financial sales. A large part of my job was recruiting banks and business owners to use our services. To do this, many times I had to go to these banks and businesses and do a sales presentation. In these presentations, I had to make sure I conveyed who we were and what value we would be to them as our client. Seems easy enough, right? Just go in, give them some papers, have a PowerPoint© with the important information, and explain those three important things. Nope. I quickly learned that my audiences were disregarding me within the first few minutes of my presentation.

Getting these opportunities to give a presentation was hard enough in itself. Most of these potential clients didn't really want to be spending their time listening to me, as they had more important and better things to do with their business time. Many of the people I presented to were there begrudgingly in their bosses' places. It was apparent from the beginning no one thought this presentation would be worthwhile. I learned that if I wanted their business, I had to have their full engagement. I needed to capture their attention at the very start, and keep it. They had to be entertained. They had to be wowed. I had to know about them, and they needed to see that. I had to speak their lingo, I had to know their wants and needs, and I had to know what made them happy and enthused. Otherwise, our product and the value I was presenting would fall on bored, deaf ears. I had to be on. I had to bring the show. So, I did. And it made all the difference in the world. The show mattered.

What does this have to do with teaching? It's the same thing. We have a product, a service, a value that we are trying to get our students to buy. It's our curriculum, it's our standards, it's our grade level material. We have to convey how our product works and what its true value is. We absolutely must be more than just a content provider. We have to capture our students' attention, build that wonder and excitement, and make them want what we are selling. We have to know them: what their interests and dreams are, how they work. They have to like us. Just like my sales audiences, the vast majority of students would rather be doing something other than sitting in a classroom. For many, they feel they're there because their boss (mom and dad) are making them go. If we are to be successful, we have to bring the show in all capacities. The show matters.

Why do we spend so much time making our homes look so festive and decorative when we have guests over for holidays and special occasions? Because the show matters. It creates the mood, the experience, the perfect setting for the magical memories we make. Why do the best decorated houses on Halloween get all the attention and all the buzz? Why are those the only houses the kids remember years later? It was the attention to detail, the visual behind the mood and experience, the fun, and the exciting lasting impression. It's because they brought the show, and the show matters.

In sales, if you're forgettable and not on your game with the best show, you'll struggle getting clients to hear you, and they won't buy what you're selling. In teaching, if you don't captivate your students, create that wonder, and build those relationships, you'll struggle getting students to hear you, and they won't buy what you're selling.

How we design our classrooms, how we create wonder, how we captivate in our lessons, how we incorporate the fun, how we get to know our students, how we entertain—it's all part of the show that we need to bring to our teaching. It has made all the difference for us, and it will make all the difference for you. The show matters.

Homework

"How should I start? My daughter Abbi just completely changed when she got to Mr. T.'s 6th grade class. Before it was just a huge struggle with homework. I am so thrilled she didn't struggle. It was amazing how Mr. T did it. It was like magic.

Right away when she got home she did her homework. She would say, "I'm on a mission." It's amazing how much she changed being in his class. I don't know what inspirational things he's been telling his students, but it's just amazing the change I saw in her from 5th grade to 6th grade. Before she didn't read a lot. She didn't read anything unless it was for homework. When she was in Mr. T's class, it was amazing how she would finish the whole book. She was focused. I don't know if it was her choice of the book or Mr. T's, but she was immersed in her book."

-Gladys
6th Grade Parent from Mr. Trebas' Class

Dressing Up

"I thought Mr. T was crazy at the beginning of the year! Why is he dressing up as a caveman? I found out they were doing lessons on some kind of ancient history. I thought it was so cool how he captivated the attention of the students. Mr. T has his customer's attention!

-Gladys
6th Grade Parent from Mr. Trebas's Class

Decorations

"The atmosphere is something that makes you think, "How cool is this? I want to be a student. The way he sets up his classroom. The music. Everything. I just thought that was awesome!"

-Gladys
6th Grade Parent from Mr. Trebas's Class

Passion

"The class dynamic and environment starts with the teacher. You set the tone of the day with the line. That's where it started. It trickles down to the students. It's undeniable how much you love your job, and you can't hide that. The way your classroom looks, the music, the outfits. That is so critically important to the kids' attitudes and moods. I never saw a kid in your class without a smile on their face and wasn't excited to be there.

The journaling was extremely important. They were able to get in touch with their emotions and feelings. Most classes are purely academic and are not interested in the students as a whole, and you brought that out of them in their journals. They got to see the best of you, and that made them better. Mr. Mercuro inspired my daughter to become a 4th grade teacher but she didn't start that way and didn't love school. It was very early on though she said she wanted to be just like him and was taking notes on how Mr. Mercuro did his class so she could do it that way. Students feel they are part of a team and a family. Then something like math, isn't so bad."

-Kelly
Mother of 4th and 5th Grade Students
from Mr. Mercuro and Mr. Ntzouras' Class

The Stage

"How can a president not be an actor?"
–Response when asked by a reporter,
"How can an actor run for President?"

Ronald Reagan

—

So far, we have discussed the many ways we believe the show matters. The quote above reveals President Reagan's understanding of this very idea. During the 1980 election, many people just assumed that a washed-up Hollywood actor had no business being President of the United States. One person got so bold as to even address him with this very question. President Reagan's response above shows us that he intrinsically knew that in order to serve as Commander in Chief putting on a good show matters.

You may have heard it said that perception is reality. Simply put, what people believe to be true is what shapes their reality. A good president must project confidence, strength, empathy, integrity, humility, and grandeur, all at once. Sometimes, like all of us, she or he may not feel like doing so, and therefore, acting the part becomes crucial and necessary.

In our profession, we too must be actresses or actors. We must project similar emotions as the president but for our students, parents, teachers, and staff. Most importantly, our students must feel and sense these emotions from their teacher. If you are happy, or project that you are happy, they will most assuredly be happy too. This happiness eventually turns into a lasting joy that students feel each time they enter your classroom. When you do this consistently, you fill your classroom with a returning joy that becomes contagious.

When you go to the theater to see a play, the first thing you notice, before any of the performers say even one line, is the stage. This sets the tone for what you are about to see. It transports you into the world in which the story takes place.

I had the privilege of seeing *Hamilton*® by Lin-Manuel Miranda at the famous Pantages Theater in Los Angeles, California. The stage was perfect as designed with both a modern yet antiquated look that matched the life and times of Alexander Hamilton, George Washington, and the Founding Fathers of the American Revolution.

I would suggest that even if the performers in Hamilton that night were the best on the planet, if they performed the same scenes on a dimly lit stage, no speakers, and out of costume, the performance—the show—would not have been as captivating, as impressive, or as meaningful; in short, it would have lost its magic.

Your classroom is your stage, and it matters.

Make your classroom walls look magical. I can't emphasize enough how important this step is to setting you up for an incredible year. My goal each year is to make it bigger and better. One measure of success that I use to judge whether I have succeeded is if students from previous years come in and say, "Why didn't we have this last year?" To me, this seals the deal. I tell them it's not that I didn't want to have it like this last year, it's just that I hadn't thought of it yet.

A continued spark of imagination is key.

So, how to create such a magical place? First, cover those hideous looking walls that typically line public school classrooms. Go to your local fabric store — Joanne's is my store of choice— and you will find a wide variety of options. Keep in mind, you may have to visit several locations before finding just the right pattern and colored fabric. I am guilty of spending hours on end in Joanne's before I finally find the perfect match. It will also be a good idea to have someone join you on this venture. Find someone who has an even better eye for patterns and color schemes than you do. She or he must also be someone you can trust to give you their honest opinion. Someone to tell you, "Nope, that looks awful" and "Yes! This is it!"

I'm not going to lie, this process is expensive. Understandably, it might be easier and cheaper to cover your walls with paper. The look and feel of your classroom will dictate in large part the energy that your class will generate. Therefore, make it feel and look unforgettable.

Some of the newer classrooms built today look amazing. However, these rooms will still need your personal touch and TLC. You will not just be spending a day in your classroom; you'll be spending at least 180 days there with your students. Therefore, make your classroom come alive.

I would suggest that you keep things pure, clean, and simple in nature. Think of when you go into an Apple® store. Enough said. However, this is my personal opinion. Your personality may be different. So, choose a theme that creates an environment that will inspire you and your students. The moment anyone walks inside, they feel something tremendously invigorating. Just by stepping inside, they need to be transported to what feels like another dimension.

There are so many unique items that can add to the overall creative culture of your classroom. The endless items available on Amazon® make setting up your stage even more exciting. You have to make it feel clean, organized, inspiring, and of course, unique.

Items such as an hourglass, light-up moon, and LED purple lights above the marker board are all great touches. And less out of the ordinary, yet still not seen in many classrooms, framed pictures and artwork can tie entire rooms together. Oh, and do yourself a favor and get a nice (loud) speaker system. It makes playing anything so much better. Somebody even recommended one year that I add a record player. After years of ignoring this suggestion, I finally caved. Would you believe that students totally love it? They do! You can find read-along, vintage, modern, and all sorts of records to play. The possibilities are endless.

The one thing that I might further emphasize is that you should keep your class simple and sophisticated. That's the nice way of saying it. Another way is, don't clutter the place.

Too many pictures, too many themes, and too many designs will ruin the whole thing. Select a few colors. You'll want to focus on predominately four or less dominant colors: grey, baby blue, light purple, and white is what I used one year. I also suggest you maintain just one border throughout the entire classroom. Again, keep it simple.

By taking the time to design your stage with care, you are showing your students, parents, and even your fellow staff members that you are prepared, ready, and passionate about what you do each day. Climate creates culture.

You'll find that soon, your students will set similar standards for themselves and will want to aim for greatness in all they do, too.

Each passing year, you'll come up with new and exciting things to make your classroom even better. As Walt Disney once said of one of his many masterpieces, "Disneyland will never be completed. It will continue to grow as long as there is imagination left in the world." I apply this same philosophy to the classroom. As long as you continue to imagine, there is no limit to the amount of creative pursuits you'll discover, and ways you can set up your stage.

Lights! Camera! Action!

Fun and Learning

"My favorite part was that each kid was so supportive of everybody else, it was a safe environment for everyone to be themselves. Mr. Mercuro let us have fun while teaching, and we still got all the concepts. Math dodgeball was also a good motivation for us to be active while we learned. We looked forward to having fun."

-Brody
Former 4th Grade Student of Mr. Mercuro

Classroom Environment

"The feeling with both of your classrooms was the same. 150% the difference was the student-teacher relationship. The time you spent doing the activities, the dressing up, they could feel that you want to be there and they feel valued. How can you not feel valued when you did that for THEM."

-Kelly
Mother of 4th and 5th Grade Students
from Mr. Mercuro and Mr. Ntzouras' Class

Quotes

"I love how Mr. N. really resonates with the kids with how he emphasizes that kindness matters, how you treat other people matters, everyone is welcome. They all look out for each other, they genuinely care for each other. If we can continue that into many adults in this world, it would be great. Throw kindness like confetti, all of the quotes make a big difference. They really do."

-Jaime
Former 4th Grade Parent of Mr. Mercuro
Former 4th and 5th Grade Parent of Mr. Ntzouras

The Show
I am inspired to be my best. One time, Mr. N taught us a math lesson without speaking. He didn't speak for like over 10 minutes. He was just writing the math problems and doing things up at the board to show us how to do the math. Somehow, everybody got the answers right, and it was really fun."

-Caiden
Former 4th Grade Student of Mr. Ntzouras

Classroom Decor
"The quotes on the wall, I can look anywhere, and I can see the quote, and I feel good about everything. 'Can't never did anything TRY did it all' was really inspiring to me."

-Jaidyn
Former 4th Grade Student of Mr. Mercuro
Former 5th Grade Student of Mr. Ntzouras

Decor

"I for sure felt that the decorations and environment in Mr. Mercuro's class increased my confidence and daily mood. The class itself was spectacular. It had posters on the walls of what we were learning, a reading corner, and we had so many of our fun and creative projects displayed on the wall for everyone to see. Some of the posters on the wall were also very encouraging and inspiring."

-Alyssa
Former 4th Grade Student of Mr. Mercuro

Inspiration Is Everywhere

"Stop being afraid of what could go wrong, and start being excited of what could go right."

Tony Robbins

There is one phrase my wife has come to loathe. Anytime we are out shopping, at the movies, or looking for old records at a thrift store, she knows it's coming when I get a look on my face. This look comes from a spark of creativity, imagination, and a little bit of crazy. She knows she will have to listen to my crazy thought when I utter the words, "I need this for my class." It is sometimes very obvious. For example, when I hold up a young-adult novel, a fresh pack of EXPO markers, or cute decorations, she knows exactly how I will use it in my class. But she has questioned my sanity when I have held up an item like a squeaky dog toy in the shape of bacon. If people constantly question your sanity, you are finding inspiration everywhere!

Find Inspiration Everywhere
I want you to try a little experiment the next time

you are out shopping. No matter where you go, it will be better if you go to a store that specializes in specific items. For example, Home Depot. Before you go, pick an upcoming lesson you will be teaching. It could be a challenging math lesson, introducing a science unit, or an introduction to a new element to your classroom management. While you are out and about shopping, buy the most random item you can find—make sure it isn't too expensive. Find out how to use this item in your class! Try something weird, wild, and crazy. Stop worrying about what could go wrong; consider what could go right. You came up with a wild and crazy idea. You tried it. It failed miserably. Did you really fail? NO! You are training your brain to see your world in a new way. You are starting to see that in order to be the teacher you always wanted to be, you never really turn your teacher brain off! This can be tiring, but once you start, you can never go back. Creativity and inspiration are addictions of all great educators.

Learn from EVERYONE

My first year teaching sixth grade, I had a group of amazing writers. I was blown away by their ability to express themselves. They could reword questions into the answers in complete, thorough, and expertly constructed sentences. I finally asked the students how they got so good. They told me about their writing journals in fifth grade. They also expressed that they wanted to go back to expressing themselves in writing journals. Was I offended? Did I feel like I was inadequate? Had I failed because I didn't think of doing writing journals? No way! I felt quite the opposite. I felt inspired and motivated to do and be better. As a result, I went to the students' fifth grade teacher and asked him to share with me his secrets, and he did.

I still do these writing journals, but I was able to do them in my own way. I was able to build off of what was shared with me, and as a result, I have inspired other teachers to try the same thing in their classes.

"In my walks, every man I meet is my superior in some way, and in that I learn from him."

Ralph Waldo Emerson

The experience described above happens to me ALL the time, because I am always seeking new ways to do things. I get new ideas from teachers, parents, my wife, and even students! Ask your students, "How could we learn about this?" And let the inspiration start flowing.

Inspiration Can Come Easy, but Implementation Is Challenging

Each year, as I catch up with family, friends, and fellow teachers, I often get asked the question, "Aren't you glad to be teaching the same grade this year? It should be easier with every year." You would think each year it gets easier. You have your same lesson plans, you know the content, you know the curriculum. Wrong! If you are a dreamer, an inventor, a true educator, from January to December, 365 days of unlimited opportunities await you.

I am never teaching in the same way. I am always mixing things up, experimenting, and trying things in new and innovative ways. While I might be teaching the same lesson plan I typed up a year ago, I might have a new game, video, or technique I am bringing to the table. Do not fall into the trap of saying, "I've always done it this way." That is never a good reason to keep doing something!

Every year, when I set up my classroom, teach my favorite lessons, do projects, etc., I have an ultimate goal. I invite previous students to come back and see what we are working on. The ultimate goal is that they see the new additions and are envious. This shows that I am constantly improving and fine-tuning my craft.

> "Take chances, make mistakes, get messy!"
>
> ## Ms. Frizzle

Embrace Spontaneity

Those of us that watched *The Magic School Bus* growing up dreamed of being a teacher like Ms. Frizzle. We wanted the dresses she owned, we wanted our own school bus that could transform into anything we imagined, and we wanted a pet lizard to always chill on our shoulder. We later would realize how easy she had it with only eight students! Eight...really Ms. Frizzle? One thing that always stood out to me about The Magic School Bus was that in each episode, the lessons all centered on random questions and ideas from both the children and Ms. Frizzle. That is a priceless lesson we should all learn: embrace spontaneity from yourself and your students.

These moments of spontaneity don't have to be centered on lessons. Some of my favorite memories with my students have happened by following random and seemingly silly requests by students. In our school, each classroom has a document camera and a projector. The way we set up our classes, any teacher can project her/his document camera to any classroom. While I was in the middle of a math lesson, one of my students noticed the number of another classroom on the screen and asked if we could project to their class. I ran with the idea and we essentially hijacked random classrooms with our document camera. I picked up my camera to show my face, my students faces and more. We started pranking other classes for about 15 minutes. We were all laughing so hard, and later, those other teachers admitted it was funny and a nice break for their students from the lesson they were teaching. Did I get through my whole math lesson? No. But I created a deeper bond with my students, and I showed them to not take life too seriously—to find fun in random situations.

Moments of random thoughts and ideas should be embraced. One of my favorite ways to review vocabulary was born out of a random thought. I have these magnet spinners in my classrooms. One caught my eye as I was trying to find a fun and new way to review vocabulary while my students were at lunch. I had the thought of putting my eight social studies vocabulary words on a wheel, similar to that of *Wheel of Fortune*. I split the circle into eight sections and wrote a vocabulary word in each piece. The students came up, curious about the wheel and spinner on the board. I told them I would explain the game as we played. I called the first student up, he spun, and it landed on "cataracts." The student had to act out the word. I then had the class write what they thought the word meant on their personal whiteboard. Once we all agreed what the word "cataracts" meant, I erased the word, and I had to replace the word with something. It was then that I developed my famous exercise review game, "Spin, Run, Learn" by simply replacing the vocabulary word with a random physical exercise. The next student came up to spin, and if he/she landed on the new exercise, she/he had to do it, and then spin again. As the game goes on, the chances of landing on an exercise increases. At the end of the game, the kids expressed it was one of the best games they've played. Anytime they come in from recess and see the wheel, they scream with excitement! Oh, and they aced their vocabulary quizzes after the game. We achieved all of this just because I thought about trying something different.

Are all these random and spontaneous ideas wonderful? Not at all! But that is what teaching is all about. That's what we were taught by Ms. Frizzle—make mistakes. I guarantee the failure, pain, and suffering you will face from taking chances on random ideas is less intense and extreme than the results from just going for it. Take a chance and tell yourself, "I need this for my class."

Growth

"My kids are so blessed to have had these imaginative teachers. All three of my kids are interested in their own progress, where they were, where they are now and how they have grown, which is remarkable. A lot of kids their age don't want to see their grades to see their improvement, but they genuinely want to see a growth pattern to see their accomplishments. They continue to grow and push themselves to do better every year."

-Jaime
Former 4th Grade Parent of Mr. Mercuro
Former 4th and 5th Grade Parent of Mr. Ntzouras

Journaling

"I want to write stories because they entertain other people and they make them laugh. When others responded to what I wrote in my journal, it made me feel good, it made me feel really happy that they liked my writing."

-Caiden
Former 4th Grade Student of Mr. Ntzouras

Quotes, Videos, and Inspiration

"I always remember the motivational quotes on the walls and those would always remind me to calm down and think about growing. Mr. N. would show us motivational videos with people that made an impact on this world, and that inspired us and made us eager to learn."

-Finley
Former 5th Grade Student of Mr. Ntzouras

Family Environment
"I definitely feel that they have been incredibly inspired. It is rare that kids are excited to go to school everyday. They look forward to going to school. They are surrounded by good friends, a good environment, and it really feels like family."

-Jaime
Former 4th Grade Parent of Mr. Mercuro
Former 4th and 5th Grade Parent of Mr. Ntzouras

Positivity Matters
"I do like Mr.N's class more than other classes I've had. Mr.N's attitude is kind, funny, encouraging, joyful, and he's the best teacher I've ever had. Before I had Mr.N, I didn't enjoy coming to school. But when I was in Mr.N's class, I was happy and excited! He makes learning fun, and really expresses all the Multiple Intelligences and different ways of learning."

-Hailey
Former 4th Grade Student of Mr. Ntzouras

Powerful Moments

"In Mr. N's class, he consistently encouraged Hailey to do her absolute best. I remember at Back to School Night Mr. N showed parents examples of high-quality work from students in past years. This was a standard in his class and what he expected from his students. He wanted his students to go above and beyond and put 110% effort in everything they did. This is exactly what inspired Hailey to do her absolute best! She genuinely wanted to turn in high quality work.

As a parent. I noticed that Mr. N would routinely write the most encouraging notes on Hailey's tests. She would have stars and words of affirmation all over her paper. This was such a small detail but something so powerful.

Both Mr. N and Mr. Mercuro are incredibly talented and passionate teachers. It is obvious that these teachers go above and beyond in the way they teach. I am confident that both my daughters grew academically in all areas and they blossomed socially as a result of being in their class.

Both Mr. N and Mr. Mercuro had an amazing ability to inspire and encourage both of my daughters, Alyssa and Hailey, not to mention their entire class! They brought a positive energy to the class; always making my daughters feel valued and special. This in turn inspired them to put forth their best effort in the classroom and in every assignment they completed. The Pyramid of Success encouraged Hailey to strive for the award in her behavior and class effort. The desk awards were also an amazing incentive.

In particular, the Royal Writer award inspired Hailey to want to write and be a more thoughtful and creative writer. Mr. Mercuro would routinely dress in "character" to help illustrate a particular lesson they were studying in Social Studies. The picture draws were helpful for Alyssa before a test. She loved the mind map assignments because they were another great studying tool and she could use her creativity in the pictures and captions. Mr. Mercuro had numerous reward systems in place, however, Bear of the Week was by far the TOP award. Alyssa earned the award four times, it was such an honor!

Hailey succeeded in Mr.N's class with her desire and positive attitude towards reading. In the previous years, Hailey had a negative attitude and showed no interest in reading. Mr. N introduced Hailey to great books and carved out time in the school day for her to read in class. He also implemented challenges which was even more incentive for Hailey to read!

Another great outcome of Hailey's interest in reading was her desire to write.

Hailey and Alyssa learned many valuable lessons in both Mr.N and Mr. Mercuro's class but what stood out the most was that they emphasized integrity and showing kindness to others.
My daughters also learned the importance of public speaking. Mr. N gave opportunities including Wonder Struck and NYU Talks to encourage his students to speak in front of their peers. Mr. Mercuro had Cal Talks and Alyssa had the great opportunity to present her talk in Honour Hall. I was able to watch her present and I was beyond proud to watch her hold herself with poise and confidence."

-Adrianne
Mother of 4th Grade Students
from Mr. Mercuro and Mr. Ntzouras' Class

Respect
"The daily journal writing and share outs made me feel confident and inspired. This helped me become a confident writer, student, and person because my writing throughout the year got better and better, and I felt more confident sharing them to the class. I knew that I could share my thoughts about a quote to my peers because Mr. Mercuro expected everyone to show kindness to one another. So, knowing that my

writings were becoming better and better, and
the students in my class were so respectful,
I became a more confident person day by day."

-Alyssa
Former 4th Grade Student of Mr. Mercuro

Royal Writers

William Faulkner

—

One of the most rewarding activities that I do in my classroom is morning journals. No matter how many events are going on each week, no matter the crazy number of standards you have to cover, do yourself a favor and never skip morning journal time.

What does a successful morning journal time look like?

First pick a quote. It sounds easy. It isn't. At least, it shouldn't be. It must be a powerful quote—from Princess Diana, Walt Disney, President Kennedy, Eleanor Roosevelt—someone who has deep insights on the world and the human condition. If the right quote is chosen, the words that flow from your students' hearts and minds, and on to the pages of their journals, just might very well change their perspective and also inspire you and the entire class to think differently. The quote you pick has the power to transform your entire day, week, or even the school year. Now, with all this pressure, you might be nervous at even picking a quote. Good. You should be taking this seriously.

Don't stress out too much though, because by the next school day, an epic quote does need to be written on the board. Where can you find some great quotes? I'll tell you in a moment.

Second, you need to use quotes that are unique to your class. You know your students better than anyone else. You know their likes, their hobbies, their interests. So, if you know that a lot of your kids like sports, pick a quote from a famous athlete. If they are really into science this week, pick a quote from Galileo. If you just taught an effective lesson on the American Revolution, pick a quote from George Washington and let them respond to his words in their journal that morning.

In my class, students know I look up to LA Lakers legend, Kobe Bryant. As a result, many kids in my class now look up to him too. Why is this? Kids begin to love what you love.

Before journal time, I give the class a little background on each quote. When I share a Kobe quote for my students to respond to, I tell the class that Kobe works extremely hard and practiced all the time to be the best that he could be on the court. I remind them that, as much as he loves basketball though, Kobe wants his legacy to be even bigger than just being a great basketball player.

I show videos and examples of all the good

things the Kobe and Vanessa Bryant Foundation does to help people reach their full potential. Then, I read the quote of the day aloud to the class:

"I enjoy inspiring others, and hopefully that inspires them to do something great. And them doing something great maybe inspires someone else that they're close to and then you end up having this chain, this chain of inspiration." -Kobe Bryant

I typically use this quote the first week of school. I explain to the students how this is a great attitude to have as we begin our year together, and how we can all work together to help each other reach our own personal goals.

Then, the magic begins.

Each morning, I give students 30 minutes to write about what the quote means to them. At the beginning of the year, I tell my fourth graders they need to write at least seven sentences. Then, as the weeks go on, nine. As more months pass, 13, 15, 20. And before you know it they just can't stop. Some kids go on for pages on one quote. It's unbelievable.

Where do I get most of my quotes? A few sources:

-365 Days of Wonder by R.J. Palacio

-Brainyquotes.com

-Google: just type in "inspirational quotes" or "inspirational quotes for kids" and then immediately, millions of quotes are at your fingertips.

As journal time ends, I have the kids share out their thoughts. After all, what good is it if all their amazing words aren't heard?

We take a good 20 minutes (at least) each morning to allow for volunteers to share out their words. Typically, the entire class has their hands raised and we end up going past the 20 minutes. It's obvious each morning how much they truly enjoy this time.

I'll typically play some epic music in the background which makes it even more meaningful. Instrumental music from movies or moving pieces that match the mood typically are best.

Then, it's show time.

The words that your students share will be incredible. These moments may just become your favorite part of the day just as they have been for my classes over the years.

At the end, when all students have shared out, I pick one student to receive the Royal Writer award. It is a golden feather that gets to sit on their desk the entire day. You can pick one of these up from a typical craft store or choose your own special award to place on their desk.

Students have the Royal Writer award proudly sitting on their desk for the day and are full of great personal satisfaction knowing that for that day, they were chosen. It's a small thing that makes a huge difference to them. They truly treasure this moment.

Oh, and one more thing.

When I was earning my M. Ed., I remember

sitting in the library reading the stacks of peer-reviewed research articles I had found throughout the process of writing my thesis. In one such article I was reading that evening, I had an epiphany. The article expressed, in so many words, that students will take their work more seriously and work to do their personal best when they know their teacher eventually will give them constructive feedback on their work. That is to say, if students know their teacher will thoroughly be reviewing their work and giving them more than a simple check mark for completion, they are more eager to apply themselves by giving their personal best.

Feedback like this is so important to children. Actually, feedback is important to everyone. One thing that I do is have parents write their name, date, and a few sentences—or even more—in response to at least one of their child's entries. This way, if they are not chosen to read aloud in class, at least someone will be reading it.

This feedback process may take place once a week, once a month, or however many times you think is a good fit for your class. Just make sure that in some way, kids are receiving some sort of acknowledgement that their writing matters.

Perhaps your student population may not have parents that, for whatever reason, are not willing or able to participate in this process. You can always ask students in the class to write at least one positive or encouraging thing in their classmates' journals. Once again, feedback is key.

Another way you can ensure that their voices are heard is by taking a few moments to read through some of their journals, and respond to their thoughts. They will be so shocked and thrilled that you, as their teacher, took time to do this, and will treasure your words of encouragement more than you may ever know.

Do these things, and I believe your classroom will be transported to the world of imagination, wonder, and inspiration. When you do this daily writing activity, soon you'll ask how you ever ran your classroom without morning journal time.

John Hattie and Helen Timperley wrote an incredibly influential researched-based journal article titled, "The Power of Feedback." Printed in the *Review of Educational Research*, the authors concluded the following:

"If feedback is directed at the right level, it can assist students to comprehend, engage, or develop effective strategies to process the information intended to be learned. To be effective, feedback needs to be clear, purposeful, meaningful, and compatible with students' prior knowledge and to provide logical connections" (Pg. 104).

For both my elementary and college students, I embrace the grading philosophy that Mr. Hattie and Ms. Timperley emphasize in their research. In fact, for major papers and essays that students submit, I return their papers with a typed letter responding to their work. In that letter, I provide specific praise for the areas in which they showed creativity, complex-critical thinking, and meaningful reflections of the work they turned in. If and when necessary, I also provide areas where they can improve.

This feedback serves multiple purposes. First, it shows the student that I do care about their work and that I will be reading it. This causes students to turn in their best work because they know that I eventually read each word they write. This pushes them to give their absolute best. Second, by providing this feedback, it helps each student become aware of how they can improve, and how to do even better on their next assignment. This promotes a growth mindset that is key for success both inside and outside the classroom.

I also print these out and sign each letter. There is something about a signature that gives it that personal touch.

Here now are some examples of letters I've written to students based on the work they turned in. I've replaced their names with pseudo-names to preserve their privacy.

Dear Walt,

WOW! I am so impressed with your legend! You clearly took great care to thoughtfully create a meaningful and magical story. I was captivated by every page that you wrote. You used suspense and action scenes, combined with imagination and wonder, to describe the epic tale of Misty the Unicorn.

I also enjoyed the way you built a strong relationship between Sarah and Misty. Even though they lived in different parts of the world, they were still able to form a strong friendship. This shows that sometimes, even distance can't keep great friends apart for too long. Thank you for writing such an impressive legend, and for taking the time to give 110%. Keep on working hard and writing passionately. You clearly have a gift for writing!

Sincerely,

Mr. N

Dear Ashley,

I am continually impressed with your writing skills. You have such a wide vocabulary and your imagination truly is magical. The relationship between Hootie and Kaeme certainly was captivating. Especially impressive was how you were able to tie both fantasy and realism together made your story so enjoyable to read. Hootie's deal with Kaeme to save him from the snow only if he would stop hunting seals, and Kaeme's inner struggle to accept Hootie's offer, added more suspense to the story. I was impressed with the new names you gave each character at the end of the story. Kaeme's change to "He Who Is An Owl's Best Friend" and Hootie's name of "A Man's Best Friend" demonstrates even more, their strong relationship. I believe your story shows the power that someone, or even an animal, can have on another individual.

More importantly, how others can change people for the better. Thank you for writing so passionately. You truly have a gift with words, and I know that this talent will continue to bring you much success.

Sincerely,

Mr. N

Dear Elaine,

Once again, I am truly impressed by your incredible writing skills. Your legend, The Magical Golden Horn, brought to life the importance of living a life that is dedicated to the service of others. I thought it was especially important that Lightning was so focused on doing good for others. When Lightning said, "It's just that I have not saved anyone or done something special" this showed that even though she accomplished her goal, she still wanted to do more. She wanted to make a difference in others.

Also inspiring was that when Lightning was in the process of saving Amy, it was then that she turned into a magical unicorn. This is great symbolism. I believe it means that, just like Lightning, when we do things to help others, we too can feel a magic that can lift our spirits and bring lasting happiness and joy. It is clear that you have a passion and a talent for writing, Elaine. Keep using your talents to inspire. You definitely have the Mamba Mentality!

Sincerely,

Mr. N

Dear Jake,

You clearly understand the power and importance of using effective technology inside your future classroom. Be sure that you review the study guide and fully prepare yourself for the content on which you will be tested. I did not see a definition of formative and summative assessments within your essay. Therefore, you missed out on earning the maximum points for this assignment. This also led to a lack of depth and complexity in your final analysis. However, I am confident that when you become a teacher, you will look for ways to help promote a love of learning within the hearts and minds of your students.

Keep working hard and pushing yourself to do great things. Your future students will benefit greatly from this and you will find joy and inspiration in your work as a future molder of America's future generations for years to come.

Sincerely,
Prof. N

Dear Linda,

You did a remarkable job organizing your thoughts and expressing your passion for integrating technology in your future classroom. This will encourage your future students to become engaged and motivated to learn the content you will be teaching them. All throughout your work, you gave clear examples and provided explanations, and properly identified various formative and summative assessments to assess student learning.

Overall, I am impressed with your written work and know that God will use you to inspire a love of learning in the hearts and minds of your students. Well done!

> Sincerely,
> Prof. N

Dear Chris,

It is clear you understand the importance of using a wide variety of technological applications in your future classroom. Also impressive is your understanding of the formative and summative assessment process to guide your future lesson plans. Be sure to include more thoughts on your future essays by extending your written descriptions. Also, rather than reusing the same word—in this case, "fostering"—attempt to diversify the breadth of your words throughout your written work. Also, beneficial for you will be to include a strong conclusion to your essay summarizing the main idea and key details from your work. Looking forward to you ending this trimester off strong!

> Sincerely,
> Prof. N

Dear Natalie,

You presented a variety of effective methods to assess students' understanding of the material using technology as a means of assessment. However, you did not properly identify summative and formative assessment accurately, which led to a lack of depth and complexity to your response. Also, beneficial in earning higher grades on future assignments will be the addition of a strong conclusion to your essay. Adding details to support your thoughts will certainly increase your achievement levels. Be sure also to take advantage of the study guides provided so that you can more fully prepare yourself with the knowledge of the content you will be tested on. Looking forward to you finishing this semester off strong! Overall, I can tell that your response indicated a sincere passion and excitement to make learning fun and meaningful for your future students. The level of enthusiasm you have will certainly lead to a great future of teaching for you, and will bring you great joy in the years to come. Keep aiming high, keep pushing yourself, and keep that Mamba Mentality!

    Sincerely,
    Prof. N

    Toward the end of one semester, I had one of my college students come up to me after class to tell me that the letter I wrote made a big impact on her life. She said that throughout her time at Vanguard, she had saved various letters and notes from professors who encouraged her throughout the years. She went on to say that the feedback I provided meant so much to her that she was going to hang it up and save it forever!

    This made all those days of writing detailed feedback for my students well worth it.

    Whether it is in writing, a math quiz, or some other assessment you are assigning, I challenge you to think about this: Are you willing to give constructive and meaningful feedback on this assignment? If so, then definitely assign it. If not, perhaps consider other ways you can assess your students' learning in a way that allows you to let them know your thoughts on their work. It's key for students to know that their work will be reviewed and that you will let them know your suggestions and thoughts on their progress.

Students value the words of their teachers more than we may even know. We sometimes aren't fully aware what challenges and difficulties our students are facing at home. However, we have the power and the opportunity each year to leave a positive imprint in the hearts and minds of each and every one of our students. We as teachers have the unique power to lift them up, encourage them, and empower them to overcome even the most challenging of situations. We have the power to cause them to believe in themselves. To illuminate talents and skills they perhaps thought they didn't have.

We just have to take the time to do it.

While the task may seem daunting, and perhaps we can't write back to every single assignment, I encourage you to start with one this year. Provide meaningful, descriptive, encouraging, and specific feedback for your students. You'll find that this experience is in fact life-changing for you and your students.

The Show

"Caiden has always said he wants to be an actor and loves to make people laugh and express himself. When you provide that platform for them with the voices, I can see how he would like that. He loves that spotlight moment. That is an outlet for him."

-Jaime
Former 4th Grade Parent of Mr. Mercuro
Former 4th and 5th Grade Parent of Mr. Ntzouras

Royal Writer Award and Supportive Environment

"I loved how we would all want to share our morning journals. I personally love writing, so that was my favorite part of the day.We would even make a game and compete for the royal writer award. It made me feel so special when I was chosen by Mr. N for this award. That gave me an opportunity to share my ideas with the class and it created a supportive environment that made me want to learn more. A supportive classroom really helped me to share my ideas and opinions, and helps others do the same. To me, when others share their ideas, it helps me gain knowledge, gaining their perspective, and seeing that others support each other."

-Finley
Former 5th Grade Student of Mr. Ntzouras

Inspiration

"I still remember the quote, 'Can't never did anything TRY did it all'. I would always wake up everyday, and say this quote, and say that today is going to be a great day. It puts you in such a good mood."

-Brody
Former 4th Grade Student of Mr. Mercuro

Decor

"The way you decorated it, it made the kids feel like you wanted them to be there."

-Jennifer
Mother of 4th and 5th Grade Student
from Mr. Mercuro and Mr. Ntzouras' Class

Attitude of Gratitude

"Gratitude can transform common days into thanksgiving, turn routine jobs into joy, and change ordinary opportunities into blessings."

William Arthur Ward

—

How Do Children View the World?

If you take a few minutes to interview a child, any child, any age, you will most likely find a common theme: children tend to focus on themselves. They're consumed by what they want for Christmas, what they did over the weekend, what his or her parent won't let them do, what phone they want, etc. Self-centeredness is a part of who we are. We love ourselves and can't wait to show the world why we matter.

How Do Adults View the World?

This human characteristic of being selfish is still within every adult, but we have either learned how to A. hide this characteristic or B. focus it on others and on the blessings we have. There is also option C. We haven't learned how to be an adult and still focus on ourselves.

Is there a way to shape how children view the world, and therefore, plant the seeds of gratitude for the future adults they will become? Can we instill an attitude of gratitude within children? Is it worth it? Yes, yes, and an even more resounding YES!

Precious Moments

Every day in class, during our journal time, my students are challenged to write a daily attitude of gratitude. It is simple. All they need to do in one to two sentences is write what they are thankful for. It can be simple, profound, or silly. Sometimes the silly expressions of gratitude lead to deeper discussions, like why unicorns make our lives better. The more serious expressions have led to discussions about why we should be thankful for our fears. The crown jewel of every attitude of gratitude is the hashtags that students create. Student journals are transformed into their own personal social media, being driven by a desire to share, connect, and inspire others.

Let me give an example.

Today, I am thankful for running water. There are many people that have to walk for miles for their water. #H2OhYes #WaterIsABlessing #GiveYourSinkAHug

Sometimes, students find themselves spending more time on their attitudes of gratitude than their actual journal writing!

The most essential part of attitude of gratitude is the sharing.

Great Ideas Are Worth Sharing

William Arthur Ward, one of America's most quoted authors said, "Feeling gratitude and not expressing it is like wrapping a present and not giving it."

If a student wants to share, let them— every single one of them. Do not place time constraints on your sharing time. You are robbing the person sharing, the audience, and even yourself if you put a time limit on your sharing time. There have been times during our journal sharing time when the bell has rung for recess and the class has exclaimed, "No! Can we stay in? Let's finish sharing!" It does happen and can happen. You just need three things to bring your attitude of gratitude sharing time to the next level.

1. *Participate Yourself*

Make sure while the students are writing in their journals that you write something on the board as well. This is a great time to express your love for your students.

Show them you care, show them it is OK to care, show them how to care. Use funny hashtags and maybe throw in a pun or two.

2. *Play Inspiring Music*

There are countless pieces of music you can

find online to download and play during these sharing times. We had the opportunity to present some of our ideas to a group of university students, studying to become elementary teachers. To emphasize our point, we played inspirational music and required students to share out. One student even said, "I feel like I need to say something epic to match this music!" Music is that little touch that will inspire the students to write something worthy of the music being played.

3. *Point out the Good in All Things*

Teach your students that there is always something to be thankful for. In an increasingly pessimistic and self-centered world, we must be the ones to teach and show students how to wrap this present of gratitude and share it with others.

> "A great teacher is a great artist;
> his medium is not canvas, but the
> human soul."
>
> # Anonymous

By taking time every day to invite your students to participate in a quick attitude of gratitude, you are allowing them to express part of his or her soul and share that with the class. Teach the future of humanity how to find and be the good. Our world so desperately needs it.

Curiosity

"In Mr. Mercuro's class, he spoke to Dylan's competitive side. Mr. Mercuro did it in a positive and friendly way, where his classmates would talk about something afterwards and would get him to keep thinking about their classwork, even during recess. This doesn't happen in everyday classes but when learning is fun and encouraging, and kids are encouraged to be curious, it makes all the difference. When you are curious you are learning. Both Mr. Mercuro and Mr. N embody the curiosity of the children and they helped and encouraged them to succeed. This focus on embracing curiosity enhanced Dylan's learning potential. Learning potential cannot be optimized without curiosity."

-Jennifer
Mother of 4th and 5th Grade Student
from Mr. Mercuro and Mr. Ntzouras' Class

Quotes and Confidence

"Mr. N also has a bunch of quotes, and it encourages you to be better. The daily journals make me feel more confident in my writing. Other people do too, and I now feel more comfortable sharing."

-Star
Former 4th Grade Student of Mr. Ntzouras

Relationships Matter

"Everyone knows who you are. You guys are rock stars. Each morning, all the teachers are lined up at the drop off line, and Mr. N. has this huge circle of kids around him. The second he starts moving, they all follow him. They come home happy. Their confidence level has completely changed. Their attitude has changed, especially with their writing. Before, when writing birthday cards, Star would ask, 'what should I write?' Now she writes so much. Dylan has continued his independent work. He has continued ever since that year in Mr. Mercuro's class. He is in 7th grade and has a 4.0. I have no idea what he's doing, but that year he learned confidence and how to work independently. So, thank you!"

-Vicky
Mother of 4th Grade Student
from Mr. Mercuro and Mr. Ntzouras' Class

Life Lessons

Mr. Mercuro often presented the class with inspirational quotes and asked the students to reflect upon their meanings and application in their lives. At one point, I believe that he even took the time to pick a different quote for each student; a special quote that he felt would have meaning for the child. Josie had inspirational quotes all over the walls of her bedroom that year. Her favorite was, "Can't never did anything, try did it all." She really internalized those motivational words. Josie still believes that she can accomplish a lot in this life if she is willing to step outside of her comfort zone and give new things a try. Three years later, Josie still has one quote on her wall which reads, "Be Silly. Be Honest. Be Kind." She tells us that these are her words to live by, and we thank Mr. Mercuro for the introspection that he encouraged in 4th grade, which is carrying on with and serving her well now."

-Karen
Mother of 4th Grade Student
from Mr. Mercuro's class

Goal   Goal

8:30 – ~~9:00~~   Journal
              9:15
9:00 – ~~9:30~~   Share-Out
            9:45 push into Math
9:30 – 10:30   Math
10:30 – 10:40   ~~Jokes~~
10:40 – 11:00   Recess
11:00 – 11:45   ~~Social Studies~~
11:45 – 12:00   AR
                    10 min
12:00 – 12:45   Lunch
12:45 – 1:30   Science
1:30 – ~~2:30~~   Prodigy   continue
          3:15
~~2:30 – 3:15~~   ~~Mind Maps~~
              Do tomorrow

Motivate
Inspire
CHALLENGE
innovate
EMPOWER
CREATE

The Script

"Mystery creates wonder and wonder is the basis of man's desire to understand."

Neil Armstrong

—

If there is one thing I know that is true about teaching, it is that there isn't a finished script. At least, there shouldn't be. In other words, how you plan your day will most certainly not be the way you planned it the week or day before. Over the years, I have come to accept this reality. It wasn't easy though. Most teachers seem to be fighting against the clock to fit everything in each day. With that comes a desire for order, organization, and an overall blueprint for many aspects for your life. This includes all things about your classroom. I get it. #TheStruggleIsReal

The reality is, I still write a daily schedule on the board. For the most part, I stay on track, hitting the major lessons and objectives for the day, if not, at least for the week. However, there is a truth that even the most ardent Type A teacher must admit: students love to be astonished by the mysteries and wonders of our world.

Embracing this truth, it then becomes necessary to accept the fact that we must leave room in our schedule for the elements of surprise, mystery, and wonder.

There are so many examples that I can share, however the one with the most impact that I can recall involves both mystery and wonder. It all began in 2014 when I showed my fifth-grade class a TED Talk: "Hidden Miracles of the Natural World" by Louie Schwartzberg. Look it up and watch it right now. Then finish reading this chapter. #Seriously

The night before, one of my roommates had shown me a video and I was blown away. I decided that the next day, I would show it to my class. When I told my students that we were going to deviate from the schedule a bit they couldn't have been more curious about what was happening next. You see, this sudden change, this mystery, if you will, already captured their attention. In this short talk, Mr. Schwartzberg takes his viewers on a sneak peek of just some of the world's most often overlooked wonders.Using high-tech microscopes, he identifies some of the smallest features of a snail's tongue, shark's skin, and the eye of a fruit fly, to name a few. He also slows down video frames to show the patterns of wings of dragonflies and how those patterns reveal that they move in all different directions at the same time. This newfound wonder recently has been studied by flight experts to see if those same flight patterns can be used in aircraft or drones. These hidden mysteries, and so much more, were further explored. Upon viewing Mr. Schwartzberg's video, one of my students raised her hand and asked, "Mr. N., can I write something on the board?" I said, "Sure." She went up to the board and wrote the following words:

"This world is full of wonder."

That simple phrase has become nothing short of an epiphany to me. After she wrote that, I took a picture of what she had written. Months later, I partnered with an amazing artist on Etsy, Laura Drayton. Through various editing sessions via email, Ms. Drayton and I came up with a beautifully designed poster with those powerful words shared by my student. Today, it hangs prominently on my marker board as a reminder to me and all of my students that our world truly is full of wonder. We only need to take the time to notice. Our role as teachers then is to facilitate an environment of learning and allow opportunities for such exploration to occur—for wonderment to be experienced. By allowing this sudden change in the schedule, and being willing to edit the script, this special moment of intrigue and curiosity was born.

After we were all sufficiently mesmerized by this incredible TED Talk, I showed students pictures of some of nature's other wonders. One of the pictures that the class was especially impressed with was one such photo of Niagara Falls, all lit up with various colors of the rainbow. I gave a mini lesson on the power of words and expression in written form. We talked about how we might go about describing such a scene if we were standing right there. I asked them what they might see, hear, touch, taste, and smell. So many students began to raise their hands to share out their responses. It was wonderful. After our discussion, I then had the students use their observations to write a detailed and descriptive page of all that they saw in this photograph. Their work was full of adjectives, similes, metaphors, and all the elements of literary greatness that teachers dream of having their students use in their work. All from this simple yet powerful experience.

As Neil Armstrong so eloquently said, "Mystery creates wonder and wonder is the basis of man's desire to understand." Are you getting it? The TED Talk that I played illuminated some of the mysteries of the unseen world in ways students had never seen. This spark ignited wonder in their hearts and minds. This wonder led to a desire to want to write and understand how to do so in a way that was meaningful.

As teachers, we have the opportunity to spark curiosity and wonder in our students. When my roommate showed me the TED Talk that night, I had already written the schedule up on the board for the following day. However, I knew that I couldn't allow that to dictate our day and deny my students the opportunity to see the world in this new and exciting way. The schedule—the script—was edited. We as teachers must be willing to allow the script to be edited, changed, scrapped, and sometimes completely altered in order to bring out the best in our students. Nature alone offers us so many ways in which to explore our world, but there are so many more. Just take a look at Brandon Goldberg's interview with Steve Harvey from the show Little Big Shots. Oh, and by the way, Brandon has also given two TED Talks, as well. At the time, he was nine years old. Go ahead and watch those now.

The Little Piano Man | Brandon Goldberg | TEDxYouth@Miami

Performance | Brandon Goldberg | TEDxCoconutGrove

Mind blown.

In all the busy things you have going on as a brand-new teacher or even as a veteran, growth as an educator can only happen when you are willing to ditch the first draft of the script and allow for imagination, mystery, and wonder.

Stay curious.

Growth

"Mr. N.s class definitely allowed me to figure out more about how to grow. Personally, I would tend to want to perfect things. It never really occurred to me how I would want to perfect things, but in Mr. N.'s class, I focused on growing and reaching my personal best. Through junior high, and into high school, it has helped me in academics and extracurricular activities."

-Finley
Former 5th Grade Student of Mr. Ntzouras

Responsibility

"One thing I noticed with both Mr. Mercuro and Mr. N, I didn't have to micromanage my kids with homework anymore. When my kids were in their classes, they started working independently. Those years, I removed myself completely. They both wanted to go to school. I had a hard time getting Dylan OUT of the classroom and would have to tell him it's time to go!"

-Vicky
Mother of 4th Students
from Mr. Mercuro and Mr. Ntzouras' Class

Personal Best

"I remember we would all have these rewards and activities and we would have bear of the week, and we would be supportive of each other. We wanted to be a leader and be our best. When I didn't get an award, I felt like I wanted to keep trying."

-Brody
Former 4th Grade Student of Mr. Mercuro

Character
"I am always excited to see the academic growth, but I am always looking for the comments about their characters. More important than their A's, it's literally building their character which is amazing that we have teachers that can do both the academic and character growth. I am so grateful."

-Jaime
Former 4th Grade Parent of Mr. Mercuro
Former 4th and 5th Grade Parent of Mr. Ntzouras

Empowering Students

"I'm right and you're wrong, I'm BIG and you're small, and there's nothing you can do about it."

Mrs. Wormwood, Mathilda

—

I want you to reflect on a time in your life when you felt empowered. Really think. At what time did you feel like your future was in your control and directly influenced by you? Was it during a service project? Possibly, a previous employer asked you to prepare and present about a skill at which you excel. Maybe you felt the thrill of empowerment as you built an IKEA bookshelf without the assistance of the Internet. Do you have that memory in mind? How did you reach that exciting feeling of empowerment? Who helped you? What possible failures were waiting to grab hold? What exciting outcomes did you experience?

The memory that you found might have been depending on your experiences in life. All of ours will be different. On the flip side, think of a time when you felt powerless. Reflect on an environment where your ideas, creativity, words, and thoughts were squelched and met with criticism, frustration, or anger. These types of experiences might be easier to retrieve based on the very nature of growing up. Often, our words and thoughts are crushed by everyone around us. Little girls wanting to grow up and be a unicorn are told by parents that they need to be realistic and stop dreaming. Young go-getters in an established company are told to keep their head low if they want to survive. In school, students that try to share their voice, take control of their education, and have some form of power are told to sit down, be quiet, and wait to be called on.

We are now calling on you, the educators. It's time for us to sit down, be quiet, and let the students experience empowerment.

Example of Empowerment

As I began my first class meeting of the year, I could sense the tension, excitement, and curiosity in the room. We sat in a circle in our multipurpose room. Rightfully named, because I brought my students here for a purpose. I was going to give them power they never knew they could have. Like a child learning about fire for the first time, being engaged, excited, and a little scared about what it could do, these students were going to be led and taught; they would learn how to wield responsibility like a stick on fire. Similar to a stick on fire, we can use the stick to simply stare at in wonder, we can use it to cook food and help us survive, or we can use it to burn the entire forest down. I want my students to set the world on fire.

Every year after the first few weeks of school, I gather my students in this circle to ask them some questions: "What do you like about school so far? What do you not like? What would you change? What are the biggest problems our classroom faces? What about the whole school?"

For some teachers, this thought of asking their students what they want to change about their class can be intimidating. What if the classroom management system you have spent all summer perfecting is not working? What if they hate the way you teach math? What if they straight out say, they don't like you?

These fears are real. Be willing to embrace them to move past the title of a good teacher. Become the life-long mentor you were meant to be.

This most recent school year, as I conducted this meeting, I was not surprised by most of the answers I received. Some said they liked the way we read aloud. Others expressed a desire for more free time (saw that one coming). A few stated there was an issue with kindness out on the playground. I was a little shocked though when a student boldly declared to me, "Mr. Trebas, you aren't fair."

Again, it is in these moments, where we come to the imaginative fork in the road in our teacher mind. Do I engage this student's response, fearing other students might join in? Would they start grabbing pitchforks and demand my resignation letter? Or do I shut the child's response down, and say, "You are a child, I make the rules, I am fair as I can be. Get over it."

I chose the pitchfork path. I asked the student, "Why do you feel that way?"

What's important to note, is that this student was one of my quieter students who would rarely speak his mind and would rarely speak in front of the entire class.

He said, "Well...every Monday, we have a competition in front of the school to earn extra recess. And you pick the same kids. You pick these kids to do all of the fun activities. I used to raise my hand all of the time to be picked. I stopped getting picked, so I stopped raising my hand."

Wow. Did you hear what the student expressed? He expressed in front of the entire class that he reached a moment in his young life where he already decided he would give up. Why try? Why raise your hand? Why try and stand out, because in the end, you won't ever get picked? I was thankful in this moment that first, this student felt like he could express his feelings, and second, he was able to do it in front of the entire class.

We were able to discuss his issue further. I was able to explain to him that I tend to choose students that are the best—behaving the best, showing the best attitude, and so on. He said that wasn't fair. I asked him what the solution should be. We came up with a solution that involved a more random act of chance with getting picked. And I will tell you, that student shared more often in class after that. He participated in group work more frequently, and felt ready to ask a few questions here and there.

What was the difference? I, as the teacher, was willing to give some of my power to my students. We need to eradicate this idea and philosophy that teachers have all of the power. I think of the scene from Matilda when Mr. Wormwood tries to shut Matilda down.

"I'm right and you're wrong, I'm big and you're small, and there's nothing you can do about it."

Teachers are afraid to let students share some of this power. But aren't these students going to grow up? Aren't they going to become adults? Won't they shape the world in which we will soon live? So let us teach them how to wield this flame of responsibility.

Community

"In Mr. N.'s class, Dylan felt inspired to think, and think through ideas and more of that community. It was a thing for him, where it spoke to him to be a part of a bigger community to help neighbors. He would finish early and help others. And he got that from Mr N. A lot of classroom settings may take that for granted, or tell them to be quiet and read your book. Some may not like that seemingly unstructured environment so they may not want them to help their neighbor and explain something to another student. However, letting them talk and work through the lessons together will help others learn, and help the students gain confidence in themselves. I know because I saw what impact this had on my son."

-Jennifer
Mother of 4th and 5th Grade Student
from Mr. Mercuro and Mr. Ntzouras' Class

Powerful Moments

"I will look back on the good times we had. I just had a good time in both classes. It was empowerment."

-Dylan
Former 4th Grade Student of Mr. Mercuro
Former 5th Grade Student of Mr. Ntzouras

Quotes

"It was always awesome to see a quote on the board, and then on free quote Friday we got to choose our own quote, and that always put everyone in a good mood."

-Brody
Former 4th Grade Student of Mr. Mercuro

Connections

"I think when students feel connections to their teacher, they want to show up and do their best work. Having teachers that care to get to know them, their strengths and weaknesses, that's important."
-Caren

Mother of 4th and 5th Grade Students
from Mr. Mercuro and Mr. Ntzouras' Class

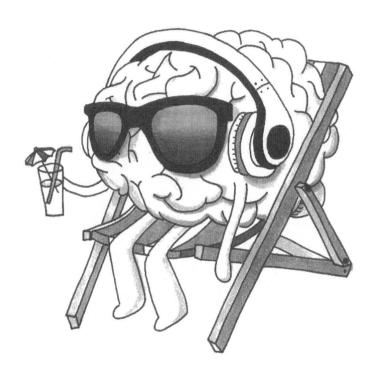

Brain Break

"A little nonsense, now and then, is relished by the wisest men!"

Willy Wonka

—

Ever since my first day of teaching, I always write the schedule up on the board. Think of it as your script for the day. I do this for two reasons. First, so that my students know what our day looks like. Second, so that I don't get too off schedule but stay on pace with the most important things I need to get in for the day.

As previously touched upon, it is even more important to be aware of the pulse of your classroom. What does that mean? It simply means you must be aware of the energy in your classroom. You need to constantly take a pulse to determine where your students are that day, in that moment. Sometimes, and let's be honest, oftentimes, it will be necessary to deviate from what the schedule says in order to ensure your students are going to want to learn whatever it is you are going to teach them. How do we do that?

Here is one way.

I recommend that you actually write the words "brain break" on your schedule. See below for an example:

8:30-9:00 Journaling
9:00-9:30 Share out
9:30-10:15 Math
10:15-10:40 Reading with Nature
10:40-11:00 Recess
11:00-11:45 Science Lab
11:50-12:00 Brain Break
12:00-12:45 Lunch

Writing this on the schedule allows for students to anticipate and know that after working hard, they will be rewarded with an earned brain break.

Now, you might be thinking, "What the heck is so good about a brain break?"

Well, as you know, all humans, including children—especially children—need a break. Do the research and you'll find that children (depending on their age bracket) can only work consistently on one thing for so long before they lose interest and focus. Therefore, giving them a chance to relax and recharge will help them become even more prepared for the next item on the schedule.

More importantly, what even is a brain break? Well, that one is a bit more complicated.

I suppose it's really anything you come up with that entertains and brings some sort of escapism to the classroom. Here are some things I've used:

1. Fill-In the Blank Jokes

First, find an awesome clean joke book. The key, however, is not just to tell jokes. It's to get the students thinking constructively through jokes. So, tell the jokes and leave a word out from the answers. Then, have the students raise their hands to guess the word you took out.

Q: A mailbox is on fire. How do you put it out?
A: Stamp it out.
(say, "blank it out")

Q: How do you count cows?
A: With a cowculator
(say, "With a blank")

Sometimes, you have to give clues when the kids don't get it right away.

When a student fills in the missing word correctly, give them a special reward for getting it right. They will absolutely love this!

My teacher, Mr. Gautreau, would do this as each class period began. If we answered the joke correctly, he'd toss us a Tootsie Roll®. It was a small reward but it was such a fun way to start class. In fact, some students would save their Tootsie Roll® wrappers and use them to cover their books or folders. Obviously, this collection of Tootsie Roll® wrappers showcased a sense of pride on behalf of the students. Knowing that jokes were on the agenda for the day made it exciting to enter Mr. Gautreau's class. This simple routine may seem small, but it was a big deal for me and my classmates.

2. Not-So Random YouTube Videos

Another brain break that I like to do is show funny short videos in between lessons. Our favorite as a class comes from a series called Studio C®, which is similar to a kid's version of SNL. Of course, your brain break can include any appropriate video. Cat videos, dog videos, America's Got Talent finales, inspiring Kid President videos, cats fighting with light sabers, you name it. YouTubelandia has got it all.

3. Student's Choice

Sometimes, I'll just give the students 10 minutes to either put their heads down, read, draw, whisper, or another quiet activity.

The options are limitless.

Incorporating a couple brain breaks will impact your day in countless positive ways. More importantly, your students will be even happier and even more eager to come to class each day.

Now, time for a brain break.

Watch
tinyurl.com/TSMBrainBreak

Draw

Take a moment to draw a design or something creative that comes to mind.

Listen

Listen to one of your favorite songs

Take a walk

Take a 10 to 15 minute walk.

Choose some other relaxing activity.

Enjoy.

Kindness

"One thing that has developed during those crucial years was that they were starting to realize that friends would be dishonest and lie, but to have the courage to do kind things all the time was one thing that was not academic. Some have stronger math abilities than others. It doesn't make people feel good when they don't feel as good as others, but realizing that being different is not a bad thing."

-Caren
Mother of 4th and 5th Grade Students
from Mr. Mercuro and Mr. Ntzouras' Class

The Show

I liked Mr. Mercuro's class because he always had fun ways to learn. The bear bucks, the games, same with Mr N.'s. class. It was fun. If school is just boring, you aren't really learning, you are just daydreaming.

I like the videos Mr. N. would share. Those helped me a lot. The Kid President videos, brain break videos. We would do videos in the middle of a math lesson. It kind of relaxed you. It wasn't stressful. It helped me enjoy the class more.

Rather than just wanting to get through it, it gave me time to process and gather the information. When you have those things, it is exciting, but not distracting and makes it still fun."

-Marissa
Former 4th Grade Student of Mr. Mercuro
Former 5th Grade Student of Mr. Ntzouras

Relationships Matter
"It is important to have the relationship. If Mr. N or Mr. Mercuro said something that was important, I would remember it. Mr. N and Mr. Mercuro would make us feel good about learning. And that was for every subject. It made me feel confident when I would say something, and say something well. And it wouldn't work in other classes, but it worked in your class."

-Dylan
Former 4th Grade Student of Mr. Mercuro
Former 5th Grade Student of Mr. Ntzouras

102

Read Aloud

"We have an obligation to read aloud to our children. To read them things they enjoy. To read to them stories we are already tired of. To do the voices, to make it interesting, and not to stop reading to them just because they learn to read to themselves. Use reading-aloud time as bonding time, as time when no phones are being checked, when the distractions of the world are put aside."

Neil Gaiman

I will never forget when I decided to make the change. I caved. I let loose, I went all in. I had recently met with a professor who specialized in literacy development for children. In this meeting, she instructed us to do all the crazy things you hear good teachers do. "Do the voices, do accents, move around, be crazy, scream, yell, whisper, cry, and go all in!" she said. So I did. The next day when I picked up *The Lion, the Witch, and the Wardrobe* in my fourth-grade class I roared, I cackled, I whimpered, and danced about, and I watched as student faces lit up with excitement, wonder, and amazement. I knew I had made the right choice when a few weeks later, a struggling reader of mine approached me and said, "I love how you do the voices Mr. Trebas! I started doing it in my own head when I read, and it makes it more fun!"

You can learn a lot from your students by the collective sounds they make. Does this sound familiar?

"OK students, take out your math books."

"Ughhhhghgh."

That collective sound, like that of a starving badger, is one that teachers loathe. If we hate it so much, why do we do things that are constantly greeted with disapproving groans? What sound do we hear when the bell rings for recess?

"YESSS!! WOOO!!!"

You would think somebody won the lottery! If you follow these few easy steps for Read-Aloud time, you (and your students) will feel like they have won the lottery.

DISCLAIMER: There are plenty of wonderful books written about Read-Aloud in the classroom. I highly suggest picking them up and diving deeper. Treat this chapter as your crash course to Read-Aloud. Once you have tried a few voices, scared a class or two, and shed some tears, Read-Aloud books will be a gold mine.

As mentioned time and time again in this book, your classroom is a stage, another world, a place where students should learn, be safe, and have fun. There is no better time for the show than during Read-Aloud time.

1. Do it everyday
2. Do voices and accents
3. Include big, large movements
4. Pull them in
5.Find a balance between chapter books and picture books

1. Do it Every Day

I get it. You are struggling to fit it all in. Your kids go to PE. You have an assessment or benchmark to give. You forgot today was Billy's birthday. A big test is coming up, and you need to review with the students. Your principal forgot to tell you Science Lab was canceled and you are scrambling with figuring out what to teach. You forgot about the parent that was coming in to teach an art lesson. Your kids need time to write. And you definitely can't let a day go by without math, etc. The list goes on and on. Your day is insane.

When the days get crazy, we try to find those extra minutes. Read-Aloud time always seems to be something that is often sacrificed. A day without Read-Aloud with your students is like eating a meal without a drink. Your day feels lacking, empty, and dry. You must find time every day, even if it ends up being 10 minutes. I strive for 30 minutes, usually right after lunch. The kids know that this time is precious. They never want to miss it, and it is the perfect activity to help them wind down after a crazy recess. If you show your students how important this time is, you start showing them that reading should be a priority in their own lives.

2. Do Voices and Accents

We were not hired to teach students what a British accent sounds like, what a pirate should sound like, or what an old lady from the South should sound like. Get out of your comfort zone and don't worry about getting the accents and voices perfectly right. You are simply bringing characters to life. You have more voices in your head than you know, and that is a good thing! Think about the countless movies, TV shows, songs, characters you know. One line that stands out to me is from one of the first songs from the *Aladdin* movie. While Aladdin sings about his struggle in life, a rather large lady with a lot of makeup grabs him and squeals, "Still I think he's rather tasty!" For those that know this line, you can hear that voice in your head, you can copy it, and you can use it. I have used this lady's voice for so many of my characters, and the students love it.

These voices not only make reading fun for you, they actually help students follow along better with your reading. As you give different characters unique voices, personalities, and life, students will know who is talking, how they feel when they speak, and actually think more deeply as they analyze what you read.

3. Include Big, Large Movements

If you were to ask any random class of first graders what the word "immense" means, you wouldn't have much luck. But if you asked any class of first graders what "immense" means after they heard your voice slowdown, and saw your hands expand slowly as you read the word "iiiimmmmeeeeennnnsssssseeee," you would probably get a lot of close guesses! This is the power and importance of these large movements.

People of all ages are drawn to large movements, dramatic people, and those that use their hands and arms as they talk. The perfect example I can think of comes from *Star Wars, Episode V: The Empire Strikes Back.* Think about one of the most important and shocking scenes when Darth Vader reveals to Luke Skywalker that he is his father. He reaches his fist out, extending a verbal and physical invitation to join him to rule the galaxy. It is a powerful and unforgettable scene! Now think what this scene would look like if Darth Vader just stood there like a boring teacher with his hands at his sides and said, "C'mon Luke, let's rule the galaxy...if you want." Don't be a boring Darth Vader! Reach your hands out to your students as you read, figuratively inviting them to rule the galaxy of epic reading!

4. Pull Them In

You will come to find out that if you have thin walls in your school and you implement the strategies and ideas in this book, your co-workers may object to your tactics. I love when these moments happen. I use them as evidence that I am doing something wild, crazy, and right! I can't even remember all of the times I have had neighboring teachers come into my room, wondering if everything is OK after a scream, bang, or loud crying was heard coming from my classroom.

The way you pull your class in will simply

depend on the book you are reading, the class you teach, and your own style of Read-Aloud. Everybody does —and should—do it differently. Just remember, the show matters. I personally like to walk around. When a moment of anticipation, excitement, or conflict is coming up in the book, I will pause, recap with the students, maybe look at one student intently with a scared look, asking them what they think will happen. For example, I was reading a mystery novel where the main character had returned home, only to find it ransacked and he saw blood on the floor. The main character looked up to see who the murderer was. When he was about to see who it was, he heard a bang.

In my own classroom, I performed it this way. I read every word, as if it were its own sentence. I revealed to the students he had seen blood. I paused, looked up horrified to my class as I mouthed the word "blood" went back to the book, paused and looked back up and asked the class if I should go on. They all screamed, "YESSSSS!" Right before the bang happened, I whispered the next few lines, paused, looked up at the class, they were waiting on my every breath, then BAM!!! I slammed my hand on my desk. They all screamed, jumped back, then laughed, as I revealed that a cat had jumped on the counter in the book. This is why we read, to show students the excitement of reading!

5. *Find a Balance Between Chapter Books and Picture Books*

Whatever grade you teach, whatever group

you have in a given year, find a good balance between chapter books and picture books. When I find chapter books, I try to find books students have not yet heard about; books that don't have movies made about them; books that are part of a series to get kids hooked; and books across all different types of genres. This can easily be done in all grade levels. When reading chapter books, it is amazing how you can tie whatever book you are reading to any standards you are required to teach. We use this time to reflect on what we have previously read, discuss character traits, make predictions, and talk about how to implement the writing strategies these authors use in our writing, and more.

Everyone loves picture books. It doesn't matter if it is a rowdy group of kindergarteners or a bored group of adults, a picture book in the hands of a skilled reader can teach countless lessons. In my sixth grade classroom, I try to read one picture book a week that highlights certain life lessons that I'm trying to instill in my preteen students. For example, on 9/11, I read the picture book, *The Man that Walked Between the Towers* to start our discussion about what happened on 9/11. We were able to look at the beautiful illustrations, talk about the Twin Towers, and have an open dialogue about how and why they are gone. Now, I obviously wouldn't read this book and have this discussion with a class of first graders, but I challenge you to pick any picture book, read it to yourself, and find either an ELA or life lesson you could discuss with your class tomorrow.

Confidence

"I think for me there are two things that are crucial as a parent. Your children are with teachers more than parents. And you want to teach them at home, but because sometimes they connect more with teachers than parents, a good teacher creates balance in who they are and who they can become by helping them see their potential.

Good teachers don't let them think they aren't good at math because then the students don't try. Instead, good teachers say, let's incorporate art and what you like to make it work. Building the trust to help them want to learn; that is a game changer. That means everything to me."

-Caren
Mother of 4th and 5th Grade Students
from Mr. Mercuro and Mr. Ntzouras' Class

Positive Reinforcement

"My favorite part about Mr. Mercuro's class was that he had such fun ways of teaching. I think that this is what made his class so exciting and interesting. I believe that knowing each day had something different in store for me, made my passion and desire to go to school and love for school spark. I also absolutely loved when he did Bear of the Week. Bear of the Week was when the student who performed the best that week and had excellent behavior won a bunch of different prizes. I remember when I got this prize. I was so happy, I could hardly contain myself. To this day, I still recall the amazing feeling of being called to the front of the room to be granted such an honorable award."

-Alyssa
Former 4th Grade Student of Mr. Mercuro

The Show
"In Mr. Mercuro's class, I love the drawings, and I still remember concepts to this day because of them. It made me picture what was going on during that time. It felt more fun. It's important because if you don't want to learn, you can't learn because your brain is turned off."

-Dylan
Former 4th Grade Student of Mr. Mercuro
Former 5th Grade Student of Mr. Ntzouras

Life Lesson

"In school, you're taught a lesson and then given a test. In life, you're given a test that teaches you a lesson."

Tom Bodett

—

What and Why

If you were to ask any teacher why they got into this crazy, insane, and ultimately rewarding career of teaching, you would get varying answers with a common denominator of change. However, when simply looking at the overwhelming amount of material we have to cover in a single school year, some can understand why some teachers fade faster than the last good EXPO® marker. This section is not telling you to avoid and drop teaching standards, but instead to find those teachable moments, whether planned or spontaneous, about life.

Last time I checked, schools do not have official subjects in honesty, integrity, social cues, self-worth, cultural awareness, listening skills, and more. Therefore, the responsibility of responsible teaching resides only in responsible, respectable, gurus! It's up to us. No pressure.

Often, the hardest part about teaching these life lessons comes from the constant, loud, and clear examples of failures. Every teacher faces them. We have great discussions about kindness, bullying, sharing, and then a day later, we get a note in our box that a student of ours received a playground demerit for calling another student stupid. These experiences will not go away. Therefore, they should not be a reason to give up, but a reason to persevere in our determination to experience life lessons. But they can make us ask ourselves. Is it worth it? Am I even reaching these kids?

The way that teaching responsibility was described to me was in the simplest of terms, yet it made sense. We teach responsibility the way we teach children how to say please and thank you. Think about how we go about doing this. If you are giving a toddler a cookie. You hold the cookie out to the toddler, and if they refuse or forget to say "thank you", you bring the cookie back to our chest and say, "What do you say?" And we repeat this until it becomes routine. After these years of training, we have hopefully trained that automatic response of saying please and thank you. But are children truly comprehending what they are saying when they say thank you? When you dish up a plate of broccoli for your 12 year-old and they respond with an apathetic and spiteful "thank you," are they communicating, "Thank you mother from the bottom of my heart for taking the time to prepare a delicious alternative to McDonald's french fries"? NO! But eventually, they will reach a point in their life when they WILL say thank you and realize that they truly are grateful for something. If these life lessons start off as a parent offering a cookie, evolve into a routine, and finally result in an introspective and reflective citizen, then we can say and realize we have achieved our original purpose for going into education.

How Often
This all seems like a lot of pressure: raising responsible caretakers of the world. Wouldn't it seem that these life lessons should permeate every lesson? The ultimate goal is that these life lessons can be taught at the drop of a hat. But more specifically, and in a more organized way, these life lessons should occur once every two weeks. They should often come in the form of a type of class meeting. If you are unfamiliar with class meetings or how to run them, I suggest doing some research on how to conduct class meetings. They are an excellent way to promote classroom democracy, further develop student empowerment, and show students that their voice matters.

But this chapter is not looking into class meetings. Instead, I want to focus on how formal, life-changing lessons should take on a different tone, feeling, and spirit as you dive into the most important and influential lessons you teach. I often begin by letting the students know we are having a Trebas Talk. They will refer back to these lessons as Trebas Talks and will fondly look back on these lessons as the most significant things they've learned all school year.

Examples

I will give a couple of examples of life-changing lessons, but honestly, I challenge you to develop your own LCLs (life changing lessons).

Reflect on those important life lessons you want to teach and think about how you will teach them. Use object lessons, involve the students, and give time for reflection in the form of journal writing. (Refer to our chapter on journal writing for more ideas on how to effectively do this!)

I would like to share two examples of LCLs I have used every year in my teaching career that often end up being emotional, inspirational, and powerful to all in attendance. Even aides I have had sitting in my class during these lessons come up to me afterwards stating how affected they were by the lesson. Feel free to use, change, and implement these lessons in your classrooms.

The first LCL I would love to share with every single teacher out there, especially those charged with the difficult task of educating teenagers, is the apple activity. It starts off by showing the students two apples. They look identical, with a few subtle differences. We pick one, pass it from student to student, and they take turns saying something they don't like about the apple. They may make a comment about the stem, specks, scars, the color of the skin, the type of apple, etc. After making a mean comment, the student then must drop the apple on his or her desk. They pass it on until all students have said something mean. Afterwards, you take the newly bruised apple and show the two apples side by side. You then put them behind your back, mix them around, bring them back out and ask the students which one was the apple we said mean things about. They can't determine which one it was. It's in this moment that a lot of students have that "Aha!" moment, seeing the point of the lesson. I then continue and explain how the mean and hurtful words we say to others may not affect or appear to affect us on the outside, but it can be extremely damaging on the inside. I then cut the apple open and show them how bruised it is. I asked them who would want to eat that apple. They respond with, "Ewww, gross! No thanks!" but I explain to them it was their fault, they did it, they need to own up to it. They start responding, "I didn't mean to! I didn't know that's what we were doing!"

I then point out that these are the same excuses we make after we hurt others with our words. The journal reflections they write following the activity are so powerful. I invite them to share their writing with their parents that evening. It ends up being extremely persuasive and memorable. It also becomes a moment to refer back to when dealing with unkind words in any future instances. You simply ask the student when they get in trouble for saying unkind things, "You remember the apples activity? How does that relate to your choices of calling Nathaniel those words?" Powerful.

The second LCL comes in the form of a more artistic and explorative approach. You start off by handing each student a blank piece of paper with a black square in the middle. You ask the students to take out a piece of lined paper and take five minutes to describe what they see on the paper. During this time, students write about the square, they describe the color, the shape, and the connection it might have to math. Some students take out rulers and describe the measurements and the area. Some students name the square. After the five minutes are up, we share what we wrote. You will find that almost all students talked about the black square. It's in this moment you ask, "Why didn't anybody write about the blank, empty space around the square? The black square is only a small percentage of the page." You continue explaining how the black square can represent life's problems and challenges. Often these problems are roadblocks of our own making, simply found in our own mind. We tend to focus on this tiny black square rather than recognizing the unlimited opportunities and potential that surrounds the square. What could potentially fill in this empty space?

After this discussion, I give the students another piece of paper with the square and invite them to turn it into something else. Students color the page, they fold it into a paper airplane, or even transform the cube into a magic castle. There are no limits to creativity. The most memorable result I saw was when a student cut three sides of her black square and turned it into a small door—a little flap that could open and close. She wrote in beautiful cursive at the top in the blank space, "Challenges are life's doors to opportunities."

Library in Students' Brains

At any given moment during school, at home, or out on the playground, it is anybody's guess as to what might be going on in a child's brain. Their imagination, knowledge, and personality are massive, confusing, and amazing. I once heard a person's brain described in the following way, and I feel it is beneficial to think about teaching in this way.

Our brains are like libraries. We are filling these libraries with books of knowledge and content. As we get older, we start categorizing the content into sections, much like a public library. Rather than a horror section, we might have a puberty section. Instead of historical fiction, we have lessons and content on honesty. By the time we become an adult, we hopefully have created hundreds of categories of mental books of knowledge and content. Even more, we have established sections in these libraries about being decent human beings. These sections might include: kindness, integrity, perseverance, hard work, communication skills, respect, generosity, and more. During a child's most crucial developmental stages, we can help them create these sections and create books that will go on their shelves. But we have to realize that the students we teach may not pull the books off the shelves until they are older. They may make poor choices in school, but that doesn't mean the lessons you've taught them aren't there, shelved in their minds. No lesson is wasted. No lecture is in vain. Let us create a generation of students that have a vast library of mental books that can be pulled down at any time of need. We can achieve this by finding the time to create and teach life changing lessons.

Journaling and Class Awards

"In Mr. Ns class, I liked the journal writing everyday. It made me feel like I had to be engaged, not had to, but wanted to be engaged. In Mr. N.s class you could earn an award, and it made me think deeper. I like the awards. It felt like I needed to do better."

-Dylan
Former 4th Grade Student of Mr. Mercuro
Former 5th Grade Student of Mr. Ntzouras

Journaling

"I like the consistency with the quote of the day. That was important. My children wrote every morning, and it gave them an opportunity to see how thought provoking their responses became over time. That allowed them to see and look back that they made true progress."

-Caren
Mother of 4th and 5th Grade Students
from Mr. Mercuro and Mr. Ntzouras' Class

Relationships

"Having different projects that allowed us to show our different talents was fun. Teachers need to work with the students helping and going over it and making sure they understand before moving on. If you don't have a good relationship with your teacher, you won't ask questions to get the help you need. Then you will guess and try to work through it instead of asking for help."

-Marissa
Former 4th Grade Student of Mr. Mercuro
Former 5th Grade Student of Mr. Ntzouras

The Show

"I noticed a difference in my son when he was in Mr. Mercuro's class. He was very excited to come to school. With Mr. N., Ava does not want to miss a day, and she hasn't been like that since kindergarten. She was saying how she can't miss school because she never wanted to miss a day. She wanted to work on Prodigy, to make Kahoots with her friends. What you teach is inspiring to kids."

-Danelli
Mother of 4th Grade Students
from Mr. Mercuro and Mr. Ntzouras' Class

Competition and the Element of Surprise

"I like the competition that Mr. N and Mr. Mercuro both had in their classes. It pushed me to want to learn more and to want to win. It was a healthy competition. I wanted to learn more because it was fun. When most people think about learning and school, they remember it as boring, but when I think back to your classes they were fun and not boring. Right now, we have a schedule and we know what is going on each day, if you know what's coming ,you can be happy or excited or not excited, but the element of surprise made it exciting."

-Katelyn
Former 4th Grade Student of Mr. Mercuro
Former 5th Grade Student of Mr. Ntzouras

The Critics

"And the haters gonna hate, hate, hate, hate baby, I'm just gonna shake, shake, shake, shake, shake. I shake it off. I shake it off."

Taylor Swift

—

As you continue to refine and incorporate new ideas in your classroom, it won't take long until you realize that other people aren't going to be as excited as you and your students are.

Why?

Simply put, people don't like it when the spotlight is on anyone but themselves. Sadly, there will be those who are satisfied with the status quo. They will be satisfied with business as usual. "That's just the way it's always been done," or "That's too much extra work," or "You go ahead and do that, I'm just going to do this worksheet instead," are some of the responses you may hear. Others might be jealous of your success. They may also be fearful that you will outshine them. Unfortunately, what they don't know is that they too can do the same thing. For whatever reason though, they choose not to.

Here is the deal.

Just because other people aren't embracing the changes you know will enhance the learning experiences for your students, does not mean you can't. There is that hope that one day they may change. In the meantime, work with them. Encourage them. Continue to try to inspire them. However, don't let them change you. Instead, keep promoting the show. Keep spreading the magic. In time, if they are willing, the stage will be set for them too.

I had the opportunity to attend a Taylor Swift Reputation Tour concert at the Rose Bowl in Pasadena, California. I was totally and completely blown away. I've been a Taylor Swift fan since 2006. She has been able to express herself through various styles and musical genres. Throughout the years, I've loved watching and seeing her grow as an artist by diversifying her talent in so many ways.

At the Reputation Tour concert, she showed quite vividly her understanding that the show matters. With more than 60,000 people in attendance on May 19, 2018, the vision she had for her tour was beyond what words can fully describe. There were fireworks, HUGE HD screens, water fountains on stage, and a flawless band behind her. Wristbands for each person in the audience flickered with different colors dancing to the beat of each song Taylor performed. She even flew above her fans in an illuminated "cherry picker" and transported to another stage in the center of the stadium. After she performed there, she walked through the crowd across to the opposite end of the stadium, while high-fiving her fans with a huge smile on her face. Then, she performed a few of her hit songs. After this, Taylor was lifted back into the "cherry picker" and flew above the cheering audience to the main stage at the front of the stadium.

It was a night I'll always remember.

You'd think that after all these years, people might just start to believe that Taylor actually is a phenomenal performer. That she has built up such an incredible fan base that loves her that they would stop hating her. That perhaps, finally, they would just assume that when she decides she wants to go through all the hard work of going on tour, that we will show up and support her like we've always done. Guess what? If you thought that, you'd be wrong.

Here are some headlines before the first few Reputation shows:

-Taylor Swift's "Reputation" Tour is a Flop

-Taylor Swift Has Changed for the Worse on Reputation-If the Old Taylor is Dead, We're Hoping for a Resurrection

-Taylor Swift's Reputation: Good Girl Gone Unconvincingly Bad

I mentioned above that I for one have enjoyed watching Taylor try new things with her music. However, many people criticize her for it. They've tried to put her down. They've tried to write her off. In fact, she even wrote a song about them called, "Mean." Ironically, she won two Grammys for this very song! My point? She didn't stop making music because of the critics. She just kept running her race.

In short, she just kept being awesome. Oh, and by the way, her fans kept loving her for it.

In packed stadiums across the United States and across the world, this young girl from Reading, Pennsylvania went on to be the greatest showwoman on earth. And she keeps on proving the critics wrong.

Here are some headlines after the first few Reputation shows:

-Taylor Swift's Reputation Tour Isn't a Disaster- It's a Victory Lap

-Even at the Rose Bowl, Taylor Swift Forges an Intimate Bond with Fans

-Shake It Off: Despite Negative Press, Taylor Swift's Reputation Tour Could Be One of the Biggest of All Time

So, as you embrace change and creativity, and as your passion for teaching grows, just know that there will be times when you are told that your ideas are just not normal. Your methods are too out of the ordinary. You might be told that you're trying to make other teachers look bad— that you just need to tone it down. You might be told that there is no way you can keep all this going, and that this is all good for now, but eventually you'll burn out if you don't stop.

Once again...ignore all that.
Shake it off.
Keep being amazing. Keep innovating.
Keep motivating. Keep inspiring.
Let your light shine.

Quotes

"Mr. N. always had quotes. I still have the book of all the quotes and my journal. The quotes inspire you, make you a better person, challenge you, make you work harder and be better."

-Marissa
Former 4th Grade Student of Mr. Mercuro
Former 5th Grade Student of Mr. Ntzouras

Creativity

"If you don't feel comfortable with your teachers you won't listen to your teacher. If you have a teacher you like you will learn from them. It's a lot of one-on-one things, when they interact and go to you personally if you are struggling. With my ability to draw, Mr. N. would have some aspect that used art or creativity, and I got to use my talent and have fun while I learned. I looked forward to the projects, and there was a creativity part that made it all manageable."

-Katelyn
Former 4th Grade Student of Mr. Mercuro
Former 5th Grade Student of Mr. Ntzouras

The Show

"Every child deserves the opportunity to be in a classroom like yours. You have something special, it's intangible. These kids will take it with them. We couldn't be more grateful that our kids had this chance. It could be a totally different experience for them. And to think that this book is out there for others, is great."

-Danelli
Mother of 4th Grade Students
from Mr. Mercuro and Mr. Ntzouras' Class

Decor

"The teachers that put in time are recognized that decorate their classrooms, that's who you are. Those people that take the time and effort, you can tell. But that's how you can tell you have great teachers when you see them put in the time and we parents appreciate that. You have made an impact on them, and they will remember you forever."

-Brandy
Mother of 4th Grade Students
from Mr. Mercuro and Mr. Ntzouras' Class

The Experience Is Everything

"Whatever you do, do it well. Do it so well that when people see you do it, they will want to come back and see you do it again and they will want to bring others and show them how well you do what you do."

Walt Disney

—

Experience is everything. In business, people pay for the "experience." The incredible growth of online shopping and companies like Amazon® have resulted in the downfall of a multitude of brick and mortar stores. Traditional stores are struggling and are fighting for their lives, with many believing it's a lost cause. However, some are still thriving. Take for example Costco. On any given day, Costco is full of customers, and they continue to beat year over year sales. Why do people still go to Costco for so many of their shopping needs that can be done online? They go because it is an experience. The customer experience is still one that creates an enjoyable feeling. From the vastness of the store, the huge variety, and the level of quality in all products, to the samples, the customer service, and the visual displays, it is an experience you cannot get online from a computer or smartphone screen. It's similar in the car buying industry. Why aren't we all purchasing our cars online and having them delivered? How are these giant dealerships still leading the way with new car purchases? It's because there is an experience involved in trying out and sitting in the actual vehicle.

People want the "experience." We remember the "feeling" we had on just about every Christmas morning from our childhood. We remember the feeling we had from going on vacations and trips. Many adults still recall and re-experience that same sense of excitement and wonder they had as a kid when going to Disneyland. On the flip side, not so much for other theme parks. That's because Disneyland believes in the experience and the show. It is their driving goal to make sure all details are covered and that the show matters. The result is that unforgettable experience. The experience creates that sense of excitement and wonder that we never forget. That experience and feeling takes us to a new world. It creates escapism. Stress, worry, anxiety, boredom, monotony is not the focus when escapism is created.

Create a classroom and an environment for students where the experience creates that sense of escapism. And most importantly, if the experience is fun, your students will stay curious and keep coming back for more.

Excitement

"When they come home and they can't stop talking about what they did. This was so amazing because, whatever they did, they could rattle on for an hour and a half, they love it so much. They love school. They don't want to miss a day of school in their life. It's because of you guys. It's like a second home. Which is why we show up, we want to be there too, we love the environment."

-Brandy
Mother of 4th Grade Students
from Mr. Mercuro and Mr. Ntzouras' Class

Fun and Learning

I was going through my closet recently and found my journal. I was trying to remember what we did and it is impacting my life now. My attitude for math changed. You made a lot of games, and we didn't know that the game was going to help us learn. I got a lot out of it because it was fun."

-Katelyn
Former 4th Grade Student of Mr. Mercuro
Former 5th Grade Student of Mr. Ntzouras

Mentor and Friend

"For me, it would be the freedom of everything. It wasn't a regular classroom that was strict, and where everyone is confined to their own space. People could express themselves. The vibes of everyone, the reading area, the books, the whole vibe of the classroom. If you have a good bond, you can tell them things. If something is bothering you, you can tell them and they can help you out as a mentor and friend, and that helps a lot.

I used to zone out, but when you listen to your students and make it interesting, I want to pay attention and focus, but otherwise I wouldn't listen, and not care."

-Ella
Former 4th Grade Student of Mr. Mercuro

Math Dodgeball
"You make learning more enjoyable. I remember at the beginning of the year you asked us to think about something to improve on. And I thought about math. I wanted to become better at it. And with math dodgeball, I want to do more math."

-Ava
Former 4th Grade Student of Mr. Ntzouras

Writing
"So, at the start of the year Mr. N. asked us to pick one thing we wanted to get better at. I picked writing. I did not like writing. Now

it is getting more interesting to me. We write about fun topics. Before I came into his class, I thought of writing as just...writing. But now we are writing about interesting things. Things that actually apply to our life. You have to think about what it means to you. Something is written on the board and we all have to think about that and put that in our own words. It was always different and in a good way."

-Connor
Former 4th Grade Student of Mr. Ntzouras

The Show

"You like to engage us with games and make learning fun, and make us want to be at school. And that influenced me in your classroom every day. If I am not having fun, I am not remembering and taking information in. I am just bored. I think the picture-draw you did, you dressing up, math dodgeball, made it a fun way to learn. It all made learning so much more meaningful.

Great estimations was another game that gave the extra detail. I feel that you cared so much about our learning and that everyone understood. You put so much effort into the lesson, the experience, interacting with us and with everyone that walked into our classroom. It made us closer. My attitude, instead of just being ok with learning it, I wanted to learn, I wanted to come to school and I didn't want to miss a day. I didn't want to miss a minute. I wanted to be there."

-Addie
Former 4th Grade Student of Mr. Mercuro

Reading and Writing Magic

"My favorite part about Mr N's class was having journal prompts every day. It let me be creative and sometimes share my own stories with the class. My attitude about reading changed a lot in Mr. N's class. I never liked to read at all. Now I really like it. He made me excited and helped me to pick good books."

-Ava
Former 4th Grade Student of Mr. Ntzouras

Environment

"Mr. N always had the candles, or the lights, and it was calming. Mr Mercuro always had the basketball frames, the university decorations, the games, and we looked forward to it."

-Katelyn
Former 4th Grade Student of Mr. Mercuro
Former 5th Grade Student of Mr. Ntzouras

The Show

"My favorite part of Mr. N.'s class is he teaches in fun ways, like math dodgeball, he puts in games like Prodigy and stuff like that. It is important to have fun because you don't want to learn if it's not fun. He puts different lessons, kindness lessons, focusing lessons, and exercises that work. Mr. N shared the podcast we made with our parents, and made it feel like a tv show when we did the podcast."

-Star
Former 4th Grade Student of Mr. Ntzouras

Listening Intently to Students

"Mr. N embraced the community feeling in the quotes. Dylan felt like part of a community; the classmates, student engagement, and YOU, Mr. N., because he felt like you wanted to hear what he had to say."

-Jennifer
Mother of 4th and 5th Grade Student
from Mr. Mercuro and Mr. Ntzouras' Class

Passion Is Energy

"Feel the power that comes
from focusing on what excited you."

Oprah Winfrey

—

Probably my favorite, and also the most important and effective part of each day is morning journal writing time. There are endless topics that can be used for this activity. Again, your passion, excitement, and enthusiasm must genuinely be known and seen by the kids here. If that's not there, this is just another daily "chore" for your students. And it certainly won't be your favorite part of the day. So, definitely keep that in mind when choosing your topics.

I use quotes. Inspirational quotes, motivational quotes, empowering quotes, quotes relating to current events or classroom topics, quotes from some of my favorite movie characters, funny quotes, quotes I may have heard one of the students say—but overall, meaningful quotes. Why quotes for me? Where was that natural passion and enthusiasm born?

Shortly after graduating from high school, I got

a job working as a lifeguard for the community pools near my home. It was a great summer job that I held throughout my college years. Being community pools, and being the summertime, kids were coming and going all day every day. And they LOVED interacting with us lifeguards.

On the hour, every hour, lifeguards had to take a 10-minute break. I would blow my whistle and announce that everyone under the age of 16 had to get out of the pool. The young kids would all hop out and sit on the edge. Many times, during this break, the kids would beg me to do cannonballs and big splash jumps off the diving board. Occasionally, I would oblige.

It was one of these days that a young child said a simple and casual quote to me. And it changed my life from that day forward. I was standing on the diving board with about five or six kids sitting on the pool's edge to my left.

I asked what they would like me to do, a "cannonball" or a "can opener." (Both simple jumps that result in a big splash.)

One child, to this day I have no idea who he was, told me to do a "gainer." A gainer is a difficult style of flip. The diver jumps off the board facing forward but does a backflip in the air. Not being a diver and filling with fear at just the thought of even attempting something like this, my response was simply, "I can't do a gainer. How about a big splash cannonball?"

The unknown child's response was one of the most unforgettable moments of my life. And it was so simple and so casual. He said, "Can't never did anything, try did it all."

I remember standing there, frozen. Realizing I did just tell these kids "I can't do it," and that I wasn't even going to try.

I thought to myself, he's absolutely right. I didn't even try. I was afraid of failure, yet failed anyway by default by not even trying. We tell kids all the time to try. Just try it. It's OK to fail, that's how you learn. But you have to at least try. So I stood there in fear of trying to pull off this maneuver, but also in clarity that I have to respond and show these kids that they're right and trying is a necessary first step to success. I have to at least try.

So, I went for it. I sprang off the end and hurled my body backwards in the air in flip rotation.

And I did it—a gainer! I was ecstatic. I felt like I could do anything. For days I was thinking about it and talking about it. I was so proud of myself.

The reason this became a life changing moment for me is because from that day forward, I would say this quote to myself whenever I was in a situation where deep down I truly wished I could achieve, go after, attain, change something meaningful or important to me, but felt it would either be too hard, unlikely, or not possible. I had to be able to always know that at the very least, I tried—truly tried. I would never have done that gainer, and may never have pursued my teaching dream, or accomplished many other meaningful accomplishments throughout my life without the impact of that quote.

Because of my passion and experiences, I choose quotes for morning journal time. Each day I use a new and great one. A student will read the quote to the class. It will be pinned up on the board along with an accompanying meaningful image. Students will journal about what they feel the quote means, how it may relate to them, and cite examples to support their answer. This is where it gets really amazing.

To reemphasize what was said in a previous chapter, as the year progresses, the students actually start using these quotes in their daily lives. Parents tell me how their child recites the quotes at home in very clever and appropriate situations. It is actually transforming their character for the better. It is truly an amazing classroom activity and experience. This is by far one of their best writing practices. They are able to extract meaning, theme, the main idea, and to offer examples as support.

More importantly they are able to reflect on a life quote with meaning and perhaps find inspiration or motivation to be their best selves and pursue their dreams. This alone would be a hugely effective activity. However, as I always do, I ask myself, "What can I do to make this even better? How can I create an even more memorable and motivating atmosphere? How can I make this an activity that is not only a highlight of my day, but of theirs too?"

This is the thing I do to bring the show, and it is truly magical: Music.

Epic Background Music

I have found several background music themes to play that have completely transformed the atmosphere during journal time. Most are motivating or inspirational background pieces you might hear in movie scenes or clips of motivating speeches and talks. I play this while they write, and I play this while they share out.

Realizing its effect, I invested in some great classroom speakers—one of the best classroom purchases to date. Music is an amazing mood changer and atmosphere booster. But its effect is exponentially stronger when the music is heard in full and felt all through the room.

Microphones for Share Outs

I used to use fake microphones for this, but I have recently acquired real ones ever since moving to a very large open classroom. Both work great. It is an empowering and professional speaker-style feeling to stand in front of a microphone with inspirational music playing, and share out your written thoughts. Even the shortest and simplest responses look magnanimous when presented this way. This may seem like it would be intimidating for your students. At first, it is. Which is why I usually wait a couple of weeks to allow the students to build confidence in this daily activity before bringing out the microphones to the front of the class. By mid school year, my students are begging for an extension in journal time, because they are writing so much more and because they ALL want to share out.

Positive Feedback

This is crucial. Kids thrive on positive feedback. With an activity like this, which can be a bit intimidating to share out, it means everything for students to get a positive response. Class applause following each read goes a long way. High fives and words of encouragement from me are a big favorite. Sometimes simply looking them in the eye and giving a gesture such as a pump fist will bring out the biggest smile. Several times a week, after the students have gone home, I will go to the desks of a couple of students, pull out their journal, and write a positive and encouraging note inside. Absolutely powerful feedback technique. Sending the journals home for parent participation can also send their pride and confidence soaring. (See Scene #54, Royal Writers.)

It is truly a magical and powerful activity when done right. The growth in reading, writing, speaking, and overall character is tremendous. And when students are begging to have journal time extended into recess, you know you have struck gold.

It's OK to Care

"Mr. N. can really relate to children. He is good at speaking to both children and adults. It felt like you always cared about our personal grade. If there was ever injustice in the class, you would solve it. We never felt nervous or scared to talk to you about anything. You always cared about the student, you never saw them as a paycheck."

-Coco
Former 5th Grade Student of Mr. Ntzouras

Public Speaking

"Writing was fun, but it would also improve my writing skills, and public speaking skills, and that helped with talking with adults because I was shy all the time. We did it every single morning, even if you didn't want to at first, at the end everyone was excited and wanted to share."

-Lola
Former 5th Grade Student of Mr. Ntzouras

Positivity

"It's the enthusiastic, positive attitude. That's what children need. You can have the best curriculum, but if you don't have someone that presents it in a way that moves and inspires you, what's the point? Your philosophy, the three of you, it moves each child and makes them think everything is possible."

-Mia
Mother of 4th and 5th Grade Students
from Mr. Ntzouras' Class

The Show
"I felt very happy, it was very bright inside. You are very passionate about everything you did. You put so much effort, so much work into everything, you are very different from many teachers I had. It was just the best experience I have ever had."

-Babbette
Former 4th Grade Student of Mr. Ntzouras

Passion
"There are two levels of teachers: some teachers who come in and see it as their job, and you can feel that. I'm in the class and I see a lot of things, and I've seen a mix of both.

You can tell, the different teachers, the ones that care about their students and go above and beyond and come to soccer games. Mr Mercuro did that, and that blew my mind because you have other things to do on the weekend."

-Brooke
Mother of 4th and 5th Grade Students
from Mr. Mercuro and Mr. Ntzouras' Class

The Show
"My attitude about science and social studies changed because Mr. Mercuro would always dress up as characters. It was more than just a fun experience. It made me excited for social studies because it would be fun for the whole class."

-Cash
Former 4th Grade Student of Mr. Mercuro
Former 5th Grade Student of Mr. Ntzouras

Magic
"Being in Mr N's fourth grade class has been one of the biggest blessings of Ava's school experience. There was just something magical about this school year and it was because of Mr. N. He was so positive and helped Ava to believe in herself. She wanted to do better because she cared about what Mr. N thought. He was constantly coming up with new ways to teach things that made learning fun and exciting."

-Betsy
Mother of 4th and 5th Grade Students

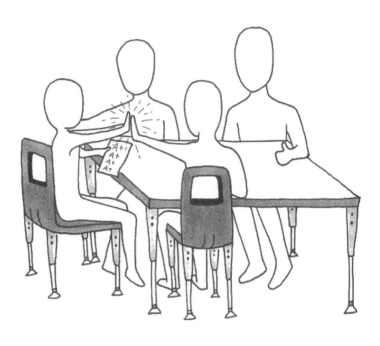

Have Fun Out There

"People rarely succeed unless they have
fun in what they are doing."

Dale Carnegie

—

Every year, I hear a common statement from parents. They say, "Mr. Mercuro, my child thrived in your class, and it's because he/she had so much fun that year!"

I feel this statement is so profound for two reasons: first, a parent is happy because their child did well. The student did well academically. They had a successful year. And second, they had fun. They did well because they had so much fun. I hear from administrators and other teachers who say they love walking by my classroom because the students always look so engaged while having a great time learning.

As a teacher, I attend several staff and professional development meetings/seminars each year. This is likely very common in most professions. And, as is probably the case in other professions as well, some of these meetings are worlds better than others.

These meetings are usually only a couple of hours long. Some occasions will be a full day, and usually occur on average about once a month.

To be clear, the purpose of these meetings is to better develop us teachers professionally, and the information presented can be very helpful in growing as a teacher. However, what I notice is that when the meetings are long, dry, boring, or drawn-out, I find myself watching the clock, tuning out, and ultimately taking away very little. On the other hand, when these meetings are presented in a creative way, with an intriguing, relevant, and entertaining style, I enjoy myself, the time goes by quickly, and most importantly, I take away just about every detail of information, and also some great presentation style ideas.

A typical reaction following a long boring meeting: "That was awful," "I got nothing from that," "What was the point of that meeting?" "Thanks for playing 87 games of tic-tac-toe with me."

A typical reaction following a creative and entertaining and relevant meeting: "That was awesome," "I am for sure doing that in my class," "Now see, why can't it be like that every time?"

A three-hour meeting can be torture with very little learned, or it can be amazing, with huge knowledge gains. Thank goodness these meetings are only a handful of times per year. Could you imagine if they were every day? In addition, thank goodness they are no more than two-to-three hours long. Could you imagine if we were required to attend for say, seven hours? Well, this is exactly what our students do. Seven hours, five days of information, five straight days a week, year after year. And they're kids!

Much like the meetings I attend, if students are going to maximize their learning, their wonder, their growth—there must be an element of enjoyment, intrigue, inspiration, wonder, thrill. I certainly don't want dry worksheets dropped on me when I attend development meetings, and I'm sure students don't want to spend their days doing the same. I truly saw the impact of this during my first year of teaching. Throughout the year, we administered reading fluency/comprehension assessments to the primary grade students individually. They were to read a passage while being timed for speed and accuracy.

Following the passage, we asked the students a series of comprehension questions to gauge whether or not they could recall and comprehend what they just read. I remember one child reading a passage—a rather dull fiction story about a polar bear, I believe. Following the story, I asked the comprehension questions. However, this particular assessment was missing the answer key. I realized that as I asked the questions I had no clue what the correct answers were because I had tuned the dull story out. The child didn't seem to recall much of the story either, resulting in a low comprehension score for that level of passage. I decided to try an experiment. I knew that the child had an interest in Star Wars and in Pokémon®. I printed out a reading passage on each topic. One was a fictional story, the other an informative article. Both were from reputable educational sites and both written at a higher-grade level than the polar bear story. The speed and accuracy result were unchanged. However, the recall and comprehension were perfect. The student learned new things about the topics he enjoyed, and showed he had the ability to comprehend reading above his grade level, being able to go back, find, and cite specific examples from the passages to prove his answers.

This same student would be marked with low comprehension, below grade level, if his reading abilities were to be based upon the original assessment. I later discovered that the original polar bear assessment had a publication date of 1998! 1998!! You know, right around when the Internet was born? In my experience, this is what makes all the difference in the world in the classroom. If the material is dry, if it's boring, if it's uninspiring and uninteresting, everything drops through the floor: comprehension, engagement, learning, joy, inspiration—all gone.

Behavior starts to go south, as well. Not only do the students need to be interested and enjoy themselves, I need to be interested and enjoy myself, too. It is this mentality that I keep at the forefront of my mind with every single thing I do. This is the baseline thinking for where I come up with my daily ideas and activities. The result is day after day of fun, enjoyment, and wonder— for me and for the students. It's the reason I often say to myself, "I can't believe I get to do this for a living." I have so much fun in the classroom with my students, each and every day. And the best part—they thrive on it.

I remember a conversation with a parent I had at the beginning of a school year. It was a parent conference. The student struggled with reading comprehension and writing in his prior year of school but was thriving early on in my classroom. The parent asked me what was taking place to cause this positive up swing. I simply replied by saying that the child is enjoying the reading and writing material. That it's fun and interesting material, and that I eliminate anything that I feel would bore me as a nine year-old kid. I told the story of the child and the polar bear reading assessment. The parent then stated that while that is great, the only problem is that in later years to come, school and life won't always present itself with fun, exciting, and engaging material.

While following your passion and never losing that sense of wonder will certainly mitigate this, that is true, not all material will be exciting. However, to learn the vital skills of becoming a strong reader and writer at the age of seven, eight, or nine the students should definitely be entertained, intrigued, and inspired. Those vital skills learned at a young age can then be applied to any material that life brings. And equally important as learning those skills through wonder, intrigue, inspiration, and enjoyment is the exposure to and exploration of newly found passions. Students discover new loves, and the creativity doorways to their future open up.

Simply put, if the learning isn't fun, it won't be effective. And the research backs it up!

• A study in *College Teaching*, a journal, found that students could recall a statistics lecture more easily when the lecturer added jokes about relevant topics.

• Neurologist and author Judy Willis showed how fun experiences increase levels of dopamine, endorphins, and oxygen—all things that promote learning.

• In a study for the *Journal of Vocational Behaviour*, Michael Tews found that employees are more likely to try new things if their work environment is fun.

So, have fun out there! Incorporate what's fun for you, and incorporate what's fun for your students!

The Show

"When I walked into Mr. N.'s classroom for the first time, I was blown away. I've never seen a classroom like this! There were lights, and quotes on the wall, and it was so energetic, and I thought, 'How could this classroom get any better?'"

-Connor
Former 4th Grade Student of Mr. Ntzouras

It's OK to Care

"I felt more comfortable, because I didn't feel like I had to do things, but I had teachers that were also mentors I could talk to. I feel like Mr. Mercuro was so involved with us and he cared about each individual student. He paid attention to everyone, but he also knew each of us. He even used our middle names. Mr. Mercuro cared about what we had to say and our opinions. It is important because if something were to happen, it's easier to ask for help because is a safe place to get the help you need."

-Ella
Former 4th Grade Student of Mr. Mercuro

Encouragement and Gratitude

"I can talk to the fact that Ava says in Mr. N's class, her classmates are very encouraging and kind to each other. Ava says everyone cheers everyone on, when somebody is going to go to the dentist, they are excited to welcome them back. She also says they write about gratitude; this is a way of being. This is a part of life. From my experience in Mr. N's class, I still remember to try hard. Kids from other classes don't care as much, but that doesn't change me, because I know I need to work hard and do well."

-Caitlyn
Former 5th Grade Student of Mr. Ntzouras

Enthusiasm

"I think the classroom environment made a difference. The quote of the day really made me happier and made me think deeper. The outfits when you would dress up, made things more interesting and enjoyable rather than just reading from a textbook. I think that the colors and all of that you wanted to bring life and happiness into the classroom. You always brought color to the classroom; you always made everyone smile and happy to be at school, and ready to learn. When you taught with enthusiasm, just YOU, I don't know how to explain it. I didn't always want to be the person that has to do this or that by this time, I wanted to. You taught me to never give up and follow my dreams. The quote 'Can't

never did anything, TRY did it all" is stuck
in our heads forever."

-Addie
Former 4th Grade Student of Mr. Mercuro

The Show
"When you walk into the classroom, there is
a bunch of quotes, music playing, lights, it
was so welcoming. It was a place I wanted to
be. There was purple and blue on the wall, not
just dark grey. When you had quotes on the
wall, I would read them on the wall during
my free time. When I was feeling down, they
encouraged me, even today."

-Ava
Former 4th Grade Student of Mr. Ntzouras

Growth
"My daughters definitely grew as students and
as young people. To preface, Lola went in a
little withdrawn, not confident, always beating
herself up about her academic performance, I
would often tell Mr. N., "Lola is not Coco."
Things with Lola, it has been a struggle,
but he never mentioned anything, but he put
her on the same path and curriculum and the
results spoke for themselves. She was a shy
student, and blossomed in a few weeks. Her
writing skills went from being able to write

3-4 sentences at best to writing full pages in a few months. She was able to articulate her thoughts. But before, she was unable to express them verbally which was huge. Now in 7th grade, she is able to carry the confidence in her writing forward, and that's because of Mr. N.'s class."

-Mia
Mother of 4th and 5th Grade Students
from Mr. Ntzouras' Class

The Show

"So, my favorite part of Mr. N.'s class was, I just remember 5th grade, it was my favorite grade I've ever had. Mr. N's class stood out because the time and effort he put in. He always made it so exciting to come in. It says a lot when you come excited to school on Mondays, because Mondays aren't' the best. It wasn't just a classroom, the classroom was special. We had reading outside, it was always so fun. It was always decorated so nicely, it made us feel so special. It was never chaotic, it was well organized. Mr. N put time and effort into the class. It was the gem out of the entire school. Kids always wanted to come to the class, even if they weren't Mr. N's student. You really do feel so special being in that class, so much fun, the wonderful atmosphere, it made me feel more organized.

Mr N.'s class was the Disneyland of all the classrooms in all the school."

-Coco
Former 5th Grade Student of Mr. Ntzouras

Caring

"When Cash had Mr. Mercuro that was the year I really saw him blossom. His confidence was knocked down a few notches, for sure, but that year Mr. Mercuro built him up; that was because of the environment, and personal relationship with the students, it was a safe place to be. It was a place of growth where he loved school again. That was huge! You would put little notes on the desks and he would bring them home, they'd say, "Who is awesome? you are awesome!" Who does that?! That year was crucial."

-Brooke
Mother of 4th and 5th Grade Students
from Mr. Mercuro and Mr. Ntzouras' Class

On With The Show!

"Be so good, they can't
ignore you."

Steve Martin

—

So, how is all of this done? Therein lies what I feel is the secret to it all. It is both simple and very challenging at the same time. With every standard, every assignment, every lesson, every review, every activity, I always ask myself a multitude of creativity questions. How can I make the introduction of this standard/activity/assignment exciting? Is there a story I can tell? Is there an element of surprise I can make? Is there a game I can create? Can I do this lesson/activity outside or in a different room? Can I build it up in advance to make the kids wonder? Are there music or props I can use? Can I tie it in with the social topics that are hot with my students? This process can lead to some epic and elaborate ideas, as well as some of the most simplistic ideas imaginable. Here are some examples:

I need an opinion writing prompt for students to practice research, making opinion statements, and providing reasons and examples to support/argue their viewpoint. What are some topics the students have a high interest right now? A lot of them like sports. Maybe I can introduce the topic outside on the field. Hmm... Perhaps the students can add their own outside team element to this based on the sport they write about. Is there a topic I could introduce with mood-setting music or imagery?

They like movies and stories. Maybe a theme from a movie they would know. What's a popular movie theme song? I could do *Star Wars* or *Harry Potter*. What would they write about, though? Which version of star destroyer is best? Is the dark side stronger than the light? Which spell would be the best to have? Which Hogwarts house is best? Ooooo...That's not bad.

The Hogwarts houses are centered on personality and character traits. Strong and inspiring traits like courage, discipline, creativity, and perseverance. This ties in with morning journal quote writing topics. I can assign them to different Hogwart houses.

No, wait! I can have them sorted into houses just like in the book! That's it! They'll be sorted into their individual houses with some sort of fanfare. They'll research the qualities and characteristics of their houses, taking pride in their work as it is personalized to them! They can work with others from their same house, giving them some collaborative time. They can do some informative writing to start, which will lead into their opinion writing about why their respective houses are best. This way they can gather information about the other houses from the other students informative writing work. I love it!

Oh, wait! Following the initial research and informative writing, I can have students meet up with other students that are part of different houses. They can get practice with comparing and contrasting, too! What other creativity can be added to this? Is there any art they can do? Maybe build/create their own wand? Or better yet, their house crest emblem. Yes! They can draw, paint, or even 3D build their own house crest! I now have it. This will be the topic and activity.

Now, this needs a show.

This lesson has to be introduced in an epic way. The anticipation needs to be built and the students need to feel a sense of escapism into this magical world. When the students came into the classroom on the day of the topic introduction, the room was lit only by fake candlelight. The Harry Potter theme music filled the room. I wore a black hooded robe and held a wand I borrowed from a friend. On the podium at the front of the room on full display was a witch's black "sorting hat." To be sorted into houses, the students took an online Hogwarts quiz. However, the show matters. I did not want them to know their houses by clicking enter on a computer screen. I needed the true sorting ceremony to take place. I was the only one to see their individual houses revealed, leaving it a mystery and further creating the excitement and anticipation. It was a great show and an epic experience for all. Through "the show," they were hooked.

Through the sorting ceremony, they had total buy-in to their topic. Over the next couple of weeks, several Language Arts standards were hit, including research, main idea/detail, compare/contrast, expository writing, opinion writing, art, presentation, and technology. The level of effort, care, and growth was seen in every student's work. It's out there. It's different than what most come to expect in a classroom. But "the show" was all worth it. And it was not difficult in the least, once the idea came to the forefront. So, why not just introduce the topic without all the candles, costume, ceremony, etc.? Teachers don't have enough time in the day to do this sort of showy event, right? In my experience, it is just the opposite. I actually have more time to cover the standards, because of the time I make for "the show." Students are almost always fully engaged on a daily basis because of the wonder, inspiration, excitement, and escapism they experience in the classroom. With engagement like that, I find I can teach any standard with the highest level of efficiency and effectiveness with tremendous comprehension. One of the very best things about all of this? *I have fun.* I enjoy it just as much as the kids. I can't wait to come to work and present these shows and watch the joy, the mystery, the anticipation, and ultimately the incredible academic growth as a result. It is truly the best.

Every activity and lesson can't be like this, can it? While I do love the big show, sometimes the idea is to simply—go simple. I often find that some lessons just simply do not need long explanations spread out over multiple days. There are many times where I come across a math standard that I feel can be introduced, presented, and widely understood in a matter of minutes. So, I will do just that. Introduce, instruct, and demonstrate the concepts in minutes. Now, where does "the show" fit in here? How do you make this truncated lesson memorable, intriguing, and highly engaging to ensure widespread comprehension and mastery? Again, you need to ask yourself those prompting questions: is there something I can say about the subject matter to grab their attention? Is there a true or made-up story I can tell that will segue into this? Or, what if I simply tell them I have a new standard to teach them, but that I am so confident in them that I bet I can teach it to them in 15 minutes? Or perhaps teach the concept without saying a word. I have successfully taught math skills in a matter of minutes without saying a word. The students watched me like a mime - wondering what I was trying to say, but all eyeballs glued with anticipation as to whether they could figure out and comprehend the skill. Not a single student was tuned out. It was so simple, yet highly effective due to "the show" of a pantomimed lesson. And again, it was super fun for me—and will be for you!

One of my favorite "shows" I add to the curriculum each year is one that I can't recommend enough. Social studies can be one of the dullest subjects in the eyes of students. It can also be one of the most exciting. In my opinion, it all comes down to how it is presented. The anticipation before each lesson sets the stage and grabs the students' attention and sense of wonder. At the start of each social studies unit, I come fully dressed up as a legendary character from a given time period. From the wonderful world of fourth grade, here are some examples of the characters and stories I created:

Unit: California Native Americans
Character: Chief Golden Bear

When the students enter the room, only faux candles light the room. Native American wind flute music fills the room from my stereo speakers. I am standing in front of the classroom, in a full Native American outfit. The students are stunned when they enter. They feel like they have been transported back in time. When they have settled into their seats, I tell them, "Class, I have a story for you." Then I begin the legendary tale:

"When I was younger and would go swimming and to the beach a lot in the summer, I noticed that my skin would become a very golden tan color from the sun. Not like a normal tanned skin color, but a very golden hue. In addition, my blond hair also became a very light golden color. Curious, I asked my grandmother one day why this happened. She told me it was because of a great ancestor of ours— a very special Native American chief from long ago.

'Let me tell you the story,' she said. 'Long ago, in the Sierra Nevadas of California, there lived two Native American tribes. The Highland tribe, who lived up in the higher mountain areas, and the Lowland tribe, who lived at the base of the mountains in the foothills. The Lowland tribe was a very peaceful tribe living sparingly off the land through farming and harvesting. The Highland tribe was a very cruel and violent tribe, attacking and taking the harvests from the Lowland tribe at will under the order and rule of their tyrant chief. With the lack of resources, the Lowland tribe did not have the strength or the numbers to ever fight back. However, the Lowland tribe would often tell fireside stories of a "chosen one" that would one day come and end their suppression and bring peace to the lands. Then one day, a child was born unto the Lowland tribe. The child was born with golden skin and golden hair. They all knew at once that this must be the "chosen one" that had been prophesied. Worried that the Highland tribe would learn of this special child, the Lowland tribe kept the golden boy hidden as he grew up. The boy proved to be a great leader to the Lowland tribe, and he eventually became the youngest chief in the tribe's history. But news of his existence didn't stay hidden, and one day some Highland tribe members spied him. They brought the news back to their tyrant chief. The Highland chief ordered an attack on the Lowland tribe demanding that this golden child be eliminated.

The Highland tribe went down to the Lowlands in the middle of the night. They demanded the Lowland tribe bring forth the golden one. But he wasn't there. He had left the day before on a two-day hunting and gathering excursion with just a few of the tribespeople.

The Highland tribe ruthlessly attacked, anyway. When the new golden chief and the few tribespeople returned, they saw in horror that the rest of their tribe had been wiped out. The golden chief cried out in anguish. His heart was crushed. He told the few remaining tribespeople that it was time to end this, and that the only way to put a stop to it all is by confronting the Highland tyrant chief himself. The tribespeople begged him not to do it. They told him he would be destroyed by the Highland tribespeople before he even got close to their chief. The golden chief reminded his remaining tribespeople that he was the chosen one, and this was his destiny. Like a great and powerful bear, the golden chief stormed up the mountains. He was attacked immediately by a group of Highland natives. They hit him with arrows and spears. His wounds, however, did not spill red blood. The blood was golden! The golden chief fought the first group off, then continued up the mountain. All the way up, he continued to be attacked and continued to spill golden blood on the rocks along the way from his wounds the entire way up. But he finally made it to the top. There he faced the great tyrant Highland chief.

Now, nobody knows for sure what took place on that mountaintop that day. When the remaining Lowland and remaining Highland tribespeople went up, they found the Highland chief defeated. He was no more. While golden blood could be seen strewn about the rocks, the golden chief was nowhere to be found. From that day forward, the two tribes vowed to make peace with each other and live in harmony. Stories of the great golden chief were passed on from generation to generation. He became known as Chief Golden Bear. Many years later, in the 1800s, gold was discovered in the Sierra Nevada Mountains. This led to the great Gold Rush in California. Now legend has it, that this precious gold we found in the Sierra Nevada Mountains is not just some precious and valuable mineral, but actually the blood of Chief Golden Bear from his valiant battle ages ago. My grandmother explains that since this great chief is an ancestor of mine, I carry a little bit of that golden skin in me."

I go on to tell the class that since this legendary chief is a great ancestor of mine, and since we are about to study California Native Americans, we will pay homage to him throughout the unit. I also add that for the next few weeks, they will not refer to me as Mr. Mercuro but instead, they will call me Chief Golden Bear. And they do! By the next day, it becomes second nature to them. "Chief Golden Bear, can I use the bathroom?" "Chief Golden Bear, can you help me with this?" It is truly amazing. They have bought in, and found a whole new love for history and the entire class culture.

I do bring a new "legend" story to the start of each social studies unit, complete with costume, room ambiance, and story. The story I use on the following unit about explorers, pueblos, and missions includes a powerful twist where the new legend character turns out to possibly be the long lost Chief Golden Bear. It is so magical to see the students' expressions!

Bringing a show like this to social studies has

made an unbelievable difference. It builds class culture, it builds student-teacher relationships, and creates fully engaged students all year. From the very simple, to the highly elaborate, the show matters. The students need it. The students deserve it. The students love it. You need it. You deserve it. And trust us, you'll love it, too! Now, on with the show!

Respect

"You treat the students the same way you would treat an adult, when the principal came in, you would be the same. It was never chaotic, or out of order. Everyone felt included, kids would see others do it and think they could do it too."

-Lola
Former 5th Grade Student of Mr. Ntzouras

Inspiration

"Teachers need to realize that they can and should be inspired by their students. They need to know their interests and let their students inspire and drive their classroom. The students know it, and they can feel it. When they feel your inspiration, they are happy. When they are happy, they are healthy too! They are sick less, and want to go to school more. It is a mutual experience of inspiration."

-Jennifer
Mother of 4th and 5th Grade Student
from Mr. Mercuro and Mr. Ntzouras' Class

Positive Reinforcement

"A person who feels appreciated will always do more than what is expected."

Anonymous

—

Positive reinforcement is so powerful. Every classroom must have a clear set of rules with a clear understanding of consequences for not following those rules. Every teacher must be fair and consistent with those consequences. No means no, and the students must know that you will absolutely adhere to that consequence schedule should any infraction take place. Then come the rewards/positive reinforcements. Doing this right may require a little investment on your part. It's worth it. Reach out to parents, donor sites, family, friends, stores, etc. to help you out with this. When done right, positive reinforcements can transform your classroom into one of the most fun, exciting, and well behaved on campus. You should have several positive reinforcement rewards at many different levels for many different reasons, and they should come out often. Here are a few examples.

Specific and Poignant Praise

Give high fives and verbal praise at every opportunity. But make a bit of a show out of it. When I am impressed by what a student has written or said or done, I let them know exactly how I feel and I show true emotion. And be specific. "You have no idea how impressed with you I am right now! Your examples were perfect! I'm not kidding, you sound like a college student! I am blown away! Well done! Wow!"

Small Daily Awards

You should have some kind of tangible reward that makes an appearance at least once a day. Usually about one or two times a day, I give out mini high five trophies for any stand out behavioral or academic act. I got about 30 of these mini-plastic trophies on Amazon® for only a few bucks. Along with the high-five trophy, I also give a real high-five. It's funny, I'll often be indirectly reminded by the students just how important these simple trophies are. If a day goes by where I just happened not to give one out, students will come to me after school lets out and ask, "How come you didn't give a high-five trophy today?" Or, "What can I do better to get a high-five trophy?" Small, but powerful and reinforcing.

Stickers and Shout Outs

Simple things go a long way to reinforce strong performances on assessments. To add a little show to plain stickers, I started using scratch and sniff stickers.

The kids can't get enough. Every "A" assessment receives a scratch and sniff sticker. Every 100% receives two scratch and sniff stickers, and I call out their full name to exclaim a job well done. I have had a couple of occasions where a parent has asked if I would stop doing such big shout outs and rewards, because their child feels bad for not having got one. I do know that it must be awfully disappointing for a student not to receive one of these performance rewards.

However, I do make sure there are countless opportunities throughout the year. More importantly, I offer encouragement through verbal praise and daily awards—and in my experience, the students who are disappointed continue to try harder and harder. And when they do finally reach that reward, it is sheer bliss— for them, for me, and for parents.

The Grand Award

A major prize should be both tough and powerful at the same time. You should have some kind of major reward that doesn't come out often but still on a regular basis. Students should clearly know what the expectations are to be eligible for this reward. Recipients should be spotlighted and rained on with the spoils. There are so many different ways to create this type of reward. In my class, we study California. The California flag, of course, depicts a great bear. My reward is called the "Bear of the Week." It is the most coveted and sought-after award in my class. It goes out to one student each week.

As clearly outlined (and reminded) to both students and parents, eligible students must be present each day that week, demonstrate excellent behavior each day, demonstrate strong effort, a great attitude, a growth mindset, respect for their classmates, their peers, their school, the staff, and show a high level of participation. Among those that do, I often need to find an above-and-beyond act or quality from that week to separate one standout student from the rest for that week's prize. Not all students will receive this award. Some will receive the award multiple times. Students and parents know this. The most important thing I must do is be true to the prize. The students must be absolutely worthy of the reward for that week. So much so, that there should never be an instance where students could question the pick.

To the victor go the spoils. The recipient receives a miniature bear that stays on his/her desk all week. They get their picture taken with the reward and are prominently featured in my weekly newsletter to families. They receive a large denomination of classroom currency, and they get to spin a prize wheel I have in my classroom. Many things can be used for this, but the wheel has several wedges with a prize listed on each. Prizes on the wheel vary, ranging from classroom currency, to table points, to a smoothie made right in the classroom, to a mystery prize that changes each week. In addition, the Bear of the Week is the first one dismissed for recess and lunch, can use the yoga ball as a daily seat, picks the daily clean up song, and gets overall priority on everything we do that week, where applicable. And best of all, the Bear of the Week gets a spot in a celebratory and exclusive "Magnificent 7" lunch. This is a special, delivered lunch of their choice in the classroom with the most recent seven winners of the award. It's a lot. However, it is one of the most powerful driving forces behind the amazing behavior, effort, attitude, and participation I see year after year from my students.

Fun

"Mr. N.'s class had a library were we could hang out. Mr. Mercuro had a green screen where we did videos instead of just a presentation, and that was fun. Both had a basketball hoop. The element of fun makes you want to go to school, it makes it better. I would say, it made me want to learn. I grew in writing because I was never really good at writing, and we did a lot of essays, but they were on subjects that were not boring. They were fun and interesting."

-Cash
Former 4th Grade Student of Mr. Mercuro
Former 5th Grade Student of Mr. Ntzouras

Journaling

"The special quotes we would write about in the morning, it was my favorite part of the day. Most teachers talk about how they would do quotes, but it only lasts a week or two. In Mr. N's class, we did them every day. I still have my quotes. 5th grade was such a special year. The lighting was the most comfortable classroom. We were allowed to eat in the class, but it was clean as well. I felt a lot more happy and comfortable in that class compared to others."

-Coco
Former 5th Grade Student of Mr. Ntzouras

Authentic Connections

"It can be hard to keep track of all 34 students, but you somehow did. Not only that, you made a personal connection with each one. The amount of time you put into caring about the students is unbelievable. You were able to create bonds, and because you kept track of every kid, it was equal. I wish we had Mr. N every year."

-Lola
Former 5th Grade Student of Mr. Ntzouras

Encouragement

"It is easy to have a strong bond with Mr N because he is easy to talk to and he cares about what I have to say. He supports me inside and outside of the class. I am a dancer and he always encouraged me and asked me how I did at my competitions. He always encouraged us to give 110% in all that we do. He still does!"

-Ava
Former 4th Grade Student of Mr. Ntzouras

Positivity

"Some things that were different about my year in Mr.N's class that lead me to a stronger student-teacher relationship was that he is fun and joyful! There was not a time when Mr.N wasn't smiling nor my classmates. In his class a major bonding experience was our laughs, jokes, and funny videos. At the end of the year, we wrote down all our memories and it took up our entire white board. Also looking back at our end of the school year video was very cheerful, but a little sad because the year I had was extraordinary, and it's all because of Mr. Ntzouras. That was the most amazing class I have been in."

-Hailey
Former 4th Grade Student of Mr. Ntzouras

Transformation
"What I saw in my child after his years with you both, was that he changed. Not only did his test scores and grades go up (straight A student), he also became more confident. He looks at classmates like teammates, and he loves his teachers."

-Brooke
Mother of 4th and 5th Grade Students
from Mr. Mercuro and Mr. Ntzouras' Class

Environment
"My favorite part of Mr. N's class was that he made it fun! Walking into the classroom each day was inspiring. There was a quote on the board each day that we'd respond to, sharing our thoughts and ideas. Mr.N played music and

videos that I really enjoyed. He gave out lots of prizes and encouraged our class to be the best. I think by the end of the year, we've highly succeeded because of Mr.N! He is absolutely the best teacher I've ever had!"

-Gabrielle
Former 4th Grade Student of Mr. Ntzouras

Relationships Matter

"No significant learning can take place
without a significant relationship"

Dr. James Comer

—

     None of this really works, in my opinion, if we don't build a strong relationship with our students. One of the most important things we can do as teachers is show the students that we truly care about them as the persons they are. That we truly care about their education, and their future. That we truly see them as individuals and get to know them in that manner. By the middle of each school year, I know each student's interests, hobbies, personalities, joys, struggles, favorite shows/movies/sports. I know who plays on sports teams (and most likely have already been to some of their games), who performs in the arts, who plays an instrument. I also know their middle names. From the start of the year, I try to guess their middle name.

     As part of my shout out when returning 100% grade assessments, I call the students out by their first middle and last name. If I have not yet learned the middle name, I make one up—which can be quite entertaining itself. In addition to this, I find myself organically creating nicknames for many of my students. What's great about this is that the other students in the class adopt these nicknames and refer to each other by them! Some, even several years later! I love this, because it happens naturally over time. This can only happen this way if I know my students well, and have built that bond. That relationship matters to them.

There are many times throughout the year where the class and I just talk. Some subject comes up, possibly off topic, and we just get into a discussion. I don't stop it. It builds a strong bond. I care about seeing them as more than students. I listen to them. I show interest in their interests. I learn their likes, their dances, and their phrases. I play sports with them at recess, watch their recess games, and eat lunch at the lunch tables with them at times. How do I have time to teach when I do all this? I have all the time I need for highly effective academic teaching because of the time I make for these things. They truly see that I care, and they respect me for that. They like me for that. They listen to me better and try harder for me with their academics. This means little to no time spent on behavior and off-task students. It is so important. And the best part is, I get to know the kids. I enjoy being with them because I have built this strong bond. I never expected this, but in my six years of teaching, across two different schools, the last day of school has resulted in class-wide tears because they didn't want the school year to end. Every single year. It was the relationship that was built. It was the memories. It was the experience they felt. It was the show.

Relationships

"In both classes, I had stronger relationships with my teachers. I could go into class with Mr. N., or go out to play with Mr. Mercuro. It was more of the energy of the class, I remember Mr. Mercuro gave a speech at the beginning of the year that the class should be a family, and it made the energy more enjoyable."

-Cash
Former 4th Grade Student of Mr. Mercuro
Former 5th Grade Student of Mr. Ntzouras

Life Lessons

Mr. Mercuro often presented the class with inspirational quotes and asked the students to reflect upon their meanings and application in their lives. At one point, I believe that he even took the time to pick a different quote for each student; a special quote that he felt would have meaning for the child. Josie had inspirational quotes all over the walls of her bedroom that year. Her favorite was, "Can't never did anything, try did it all." She really internalized those motivational words. Josie still believes that she can accomplish a lot in this life if she is willing to step outside of her comfort zone and give new things a try. Three years later, Josie still has one quote on her wall which reads, "Be Silly. Be Honest. Be Kind." She tells us that these are her words to live by, and we thank Mr. Mercuro for the introspection that he encouraged in 4th grade, which is carrying on with and serving her well now."

-Karen
Mother of 4th Grade Student
from Mr. Mercuro's class

The Show

"I have so many memories that I made during my year with Mr. Mercuro that I look back and smile on. One of the memories that I enjoy most was when I would come into the classroom in the morning and see the lights turned off and candles acting as a light source surrounding the room. I would then see Mr. Mercuro dressed as a character from our Social Studies lesson. This always made me wonder what our next lesson was going to be on. In addition, Mr. Mercuro did something called picture draws. These were what we used to study for any tests. Picture draws was when Mr. Mercuro would give a recap of our lesson by drawing pictures on the board. I had so many wonderful times in Mr. Mercuro's class."

-Alyssa
Former 4th Grade Student of Mr. Mercuro

Attitude

"I think being in Mr.N's class really impacted me and my attitude changed completely in the writing category. Journaling every day made me feel good and even writing assignments made me feel upbeat and happy."

-Gabrielle
Former 4th Grade Student of Mr. Ntzouras

The Show

"Our classroom was the BEST! Mr N had LED lights all around the front of the room. We had a couch. We had quotes all over the walls. We also had really cool awards that he would hand out every day. It was fun to get an award because it could sit on your desk all day and everyone saw it. I was always excited to go to school when Mr N was my teacher."

-Ava
Former 4th Grade Student of Mr. Ntzouras

It's OK To Care

"That year was, without a doubt, Josie's favorite year of school to date! Luckily, Josie still carries her fond memories of Mr. Mercuro with her, and the lessons she learned in his class continue to serve her well as she navigates her way through middle school.

Mr. Mercuro created a very positive and supportive environment in his classroom. He encouraged self-expression, and the kids felt safe enough in his class to really do just that…to freely express themselves. Perhaps this was because Mr. Mercuro would do the same when he came to class dressed as "Chief Golden Bear" when they studied Native Americans, or "Father Alcalde," when they studied the California Missions.

The students had such a camaraderie with each other and with Mr. Mercuro, and they enjoyed learning together as a group. The thing that stands out the most for me, and the 4th grade activity I will NEVER forget relates to the kids' root word studies. Each week, the students could choose from a variety of activities to demonstrate their mastery of Greek and Latin root words. Josie chose to create a talk show that she called, "Root Words with Josie." She assumed the persona of a British talk show host, and she would come up with different topics and storylines incorporating her root words each week. The talk show was ridiculous, but it was well received by her classmates and Mr. Mercuro made her feel like she was a superstar. She could not wait to start writing the next episode immediately after she completed a "show" in class. My husband and I could not believe that she was willing to stand up in front of the class and become this character week after week. Josie had always been an outgoing kid, but we had never seen her willing to put herself out there in front of her peers like she did in Mr. Mercuro's class. I attribute this entirely to the encouraging environment Mr. Mercuro created, because she has never done anything quite so bold since."

-Karen
Mother of 4th Grade Student
from Mr. Mercuro's class

Inspiration

"Mr. N made me feel inspired by his quotes, music and attitude. He taught me that I can achieve anything I set my mind to. He constantly filled our room with inspiring videos and quotes. This encouraged me to try my best in everything I do."

-Hailey
Former 4th Grade Student of Mr. Ntzouras

Journaling

"I think journals and share outs are really inspiring and are a good way to start the day. Journals have encouraged me and influenced me, and now I enjoy writing. It has also given me lots of practice sharing my ideas. I was nervous to speak in front of the class. In

Mr.N's class I had practice and got familiar with speaking. Now, I love to speak in front of people and share my ideas! I enjoy sharing journals and other things that let me express myself. Also debating is something really fun that we got the privilege to do."

-Hailey
Former 4th Grade Student of Mr. Ntzouras

Math and Magic

"My attitude with math, well, I never struggled, but I never really looked forward to it. It was always so black and white and straight forward. We usually worked in textbooks. In Mr. Mercuro's class though, I got to experience math in a whole new way. Great estimations, everyone could participate and have the same chance. Whether you were good or bad. In my writing, I would always look around my environment to get ideas. Having a classroom with so many decorations, with good vibes, opened so many more ideas, especially for me with writing."

-Ella
Former 4th Grade Student of Mr. Mercuro

The Secret Ingredient

"Creativity takes courage."

Henri Matisse

—

I want to stop at this point to touch upon a subject that is difficult to define: creativity. In all that we do as teachers, the most important aspect to making our lessons memorable, and therefore, meaningful for our students, is the infusion of creativity into our classrooms. As you read that last sentence, you may have thought to yourself something similar to these responses:

RESPONSE ONE

I agree, creativity is key. I am creative and always try to think outside the box.

RESPONSE TWO

I agree, but other people are way more creative than I am.

RESPONSE THREE
I agree, but I just don't have what it takes to be a creative person.

RESPONSE FOUR
I agree, but I'm not creative. I never will be.

Here is the thing. Your thoughts become your actions. What you believe about yourself, you become. I know it sounds cliché, but it is true. If you wake up every morning and speak negative thoughts over yourself, and to yourself, thoughts that remind you of all the things you can't do, don't be surprised when your thoughts become your reality. What you think about you bring about.

I have a bulletin board in my classroom with a large golden-framed mirror I picked up from Target. I used a dry erase marker to write in big bold letters "YOU ARE TALENTED."

This was strategically written right in the middle of the mirror. This way, when students walk by it each day, they see themselves in the mirror, and upon it, their own reflection. On the sides of this golden mirror, on purple glittered die-cut letters spells out the phrase

Change your words, change your world. Words matter.

Even if you truly believe you are not creative, don't go around telling yourself that. Especially don't go around telling other people that. This will only reinforce that negative picture you are painting of yourself. Instead, I'd like to offer a simple yet powerful solution. I caution you not to confuse the word simple with easy. What I'm about to suggest is simple but may require some hard retraining of your mind.

First, I want to say from the outset that I believe that everyone, yes, everyone, is creative. By that I mean that I believe everyone has the capacity to be creative. It is up to each of you to believe it. Again, what you think about, you bring about. For some of you reading this chapter, you have already convinced yourself that you are creative. You don't require any retraining of your mind because you already know this to be true about yourself. If so, perhaps this chapter is a great reminder to stay in this frame of mind. For others, this may be the first time you actually thought that labeling yourself as a creative person is actually possible. It is possible, and you are creative. Now, you've got to believe it.

Many times, and for various reasons, people allow others' opinions to define who they are. Instead of listening to that inner voice inside that tells you they are wrong, you allow the negative influences to take control. You allow those thoughts from classmates from perhaps decades ago to still haunt you. Perhaps it was a family member, a teacher, a coworker, or even a close friend, who once told you that you weren't creative, inspiring, or in some way put you down. Words have power to shape our entire future so make sure you agree with those who uplift and encourage you.

Surround yourself with positive energy and people who will help you to shine.

If you are having a difficult time believing that you are creative, perhaps it might be well for you to read some biographies of a wide variety of inspiring world-changing innovators; people who challenged the status quo—people like Walt Disney, Steve Jobs, Princess Diana, Margaret Thatcher, Oprah Winfrey, Ellen Degeneres, Robert Kennedy, and so many others.

Truth be told, I used to be someone who didn't consider myself to be at all creative. I thought that description belonged to other people far smarter than I ever could dream to be. However, I began to realize that my negative mindset was only holding me back. I started listening to an inspirational speaker who caused me to think differently about my own abilities. Once I did that, I realized that my true potential had not yet been released. In elementary school, I struggled with my grades because I told myself that I wasn't smart. That I would always fail. That I just wasn't smart like the other kids. Like I mentioned at the start of this book, it got so bad that my parents took me out of traditional school and homeschooled me throughout junior high school. Fast forward many years later, and with my newfound mindset, I ended up graduating with a Master's in Education with a 3.9 GPA. What was the difference? I changed my words. My world was changed.

Creativity can mean many things. I think for teachers it means that we are continually working and thinking of ways we can make our lessons engaging, exciting, memorable, meaningful, and worthwhile for our students. Sometimes, this process can take hours for one lesson. Other times, it comes to us quickly. I'll give you an example.

My dad and I are huge fans of Kobe Bryant. I spent my childhood watching Laker games with my dad on TV. We watched as Kobe broke records each year. One of my favorite memories I have is of Kobe's last game as an NBA player when he scored 60 points. What an epic end to his incredible 20-year career as a Laker. Now that Kobe is retired, he has gone on to win an Oscar for his short film, Dear Basketball, is an author, and most recently, began a new podcast called The Punies©. The Punies© is a weekly series with a cast of characters that enjoy playing sports together while learning important life lessons. One day, I received a text message from my dad who first told me of The Punies©. I listened to it and afterward, immediately knew that I wanted to somehow incorporate this into my classroom. I didn't know how just yet, but I knew there was some creative outlet waiting to be found.

After hours of thinking and working at Starbucks, I eventually came up with some ideas. I decided that I would have my students listen to the first episode, and as they listened, I would have them write down at least 10 key details from the story. Then, I would have them use these key details to write a summary of the episode and discuss what they believed the main idea was from what they had heard. Here in California, one of the main concepts fourth graders need to know is how to be able to identify the main idea of a text by simply listening to a story. So, I thought, what better way to engage students in this process than to have them listen to a podcast created by Kobe Bryant?

So, I did exactly that.

Turns out, they loved it. Since then, I've created various lesson plans, activities, and templates to help support the understanding of various Common Core State Standards that are reinforced by our weekly episode of The Punies©.

Here is the crazy part—The Punies© team found out that I was using this in my classroom. Kobe found out, too! The entire Punies team and Kobe ended up visiting my classroom to see the students in action!

When Kobe came, various district officials joined us, too. In fact, the story was all over the news. Entertainment Tonight© was there and captured these special moments on camera. The Orange County Superintendent was invited as a special guest for the occasion. After the event, we started a conversation, and he began to ask questions of the different things I do to engage my students. He was impressed with the various teaching strategies I use in my classroom—many of which are included within the pages of this book.

Here are some of the things Kobe said that day when he visited my classroom, as quoted in the Entertainment Tonight© Exclusive Interview.

"They have a really great teacher who is committed to teaching young kids and inspiring them. It's the teacher, that plays such an important role that tends to get overlooked in our society. It's such a huge responsibility but he's done a phenomenal job inspiring his kids."

"Do you realize how cool your classroom is? It is super cool. Ridiculously cool."

"The most important people I've found in my life are family, teachers, and coaches."

"Seeing their (students') face light up to something that's entertaining, or an idea that they capture, or you see their imagination working; it's enjoyable to be around."

Even as I type this, I still get goosebumps knowing that Kobe Bryant—my hero since childhood—visited my classroom and complimented and validated the work I do as a teacher. It will be a day I will always treasure the rest of my life. Kobe genuinely was interested in, and eagerly listened to my students as they presented their Punies© projects they worked so hard on. They had no idea he was coming that day. We kept it a big surprise. My students will certainly never forget the powerful moments we all shared together.

Creativity + purposeful planning = magical moments.

I guess what I'm trying to say is once you realize that you are in fact creative, the possibilities are endless. Never limit yourself to thinking that something can't turn into a lesson for your students. Chances are, it can!

Think of the things you are passionate about and turn those events, stories, or life experiences into lessons your students will enjoy.

Take chances. Think of the ways you can capture your students' imagination. As you do this, I encourage you to do the following:

Think big.

Think creative.

Think unique.

Think inspiring.

Think escapism.

Think powerful.

Think magical.

Think differently.

Now, be prepared for creativity and wonder to take over your class. You and your students will never be the same again.

Oh, and one more thing.

We'll leave you with one last quote from Steve Jobs. Remember, it isn't crazy to think that you can truly change the world. As stated earlier, you can. Not only can you change the world, you can change it many times over. You can change the worlds of literally hundreds and perhaps thousands of students. You are a world changer. That's why you entered this profession in the first place.

"When you grow up you tend to get told that the world is the way it is and your life is just to live your life inside the world. Try not to bash into the walls too much. Try to have a nice family life, have fun, save a little money. That's a very limited life. Life can be much broader once you discover one simple fact: Everything around you that you call life was made up by people that were no smarter than you. And you can change it, you can influence it...Once you learn that, you'll never be the same again."

Steve Jobs

Made in the USA
Las Vegas, NV
23 July 2022